Changing Days

Developing new daytime opportunities with people who have learning difficulties

Edited by Alison Wertheimer

NATIONAL DEVELOPMENT TEAM

Published by
King's Fund Publishing
11–13 Cavendish Square
London W1M 0AN

© King's Fund 1996

First published 1996
Reprinted 1996, 1998

ISBN 1 85717 106 3

A CIP catalogue record for this book is available from the British Library

Distributed by Grantham Book Services Limited
Isaac Newton Way
Alma Park Industrial Estate
GRANTHAM
Lincolnshire
NG31 9SD
Tel: 01476 541 080
Fax: 01476 541 061

Printed and bound in Great Britain by The Cromwell Press, Melksham, Wiltshire

Contents

Preface

In July 1993, the King's Fund undertook a national consultation exercise on trends in services for people with learning disabilities. Out of this came agreement that work on developing day opportunities was a priority.

A partnership was formed between the National Development Team and the King's Fund and funding for three years was obtained from the Gatsby Charitable Foundation and the Joseph Rowntree Foundation. Work on Changing Days began in December 1994.

The work is based on the belief that:

- people with learning disabilities have the ability to become full members of their local communities;
- better day-time opportunity can be achieved by working in partnership with users, carers and staff in planning and shaping the future;
- the future for people with learning disabilities should be away from segregated day centres and building-based services towards people with learning disabilities being given support to participate in ordinary activities in the community;
- the emphasis should be on developing adult education, employment and meaningful leisure pursuits outside of segregated services.

A key theme is partnership with users, carers, staff and the local community. Without this partnership, real change will be difficult to achieve.

Five development sites were chosen which had demonstrated their commitment to develop their services in this way:

    Cambridgeshire County Council
    Ely Hospital, Cardiff Community Healthcare Trust
    Hackney Social Services
    Hereford Single Agency Purchasing Project
    South & East Belfast Health and Social Services Trust.

Throughout the life of this three-year initiative, there will be seminars, action learning sets, conferences and publications to disseminate lessons learned from work in the five sites.

About this publication

This publication brings together current ideas on how best to achieve the aims of the Changing Days project. It is for anyone interested in helping people with learning difficulties improve the quality of their lives. In particular, we hope it will be a tool for managers responsible for day opportunities – both purchasers and providers. It has been designed to be helpful to all stakeholders, including people who use services and their families.

It begins with a brief executive summary followed by a more detailed but easy-to-read summary. Each chapter focuses on a specific area giving pointers for managers, staff, users and carers.

The terms 'people with learning difficulties' and 'people with learning disabilities' have been used interchangeably in this publication.

This book has been written through the combined efforts of all the contributors listed on pages ix–xi. We are grateful for their generosity in contributing so much of their time and experience to compiling this vision of day opportunities for people with learning disabilities.

Particular thanks go to Simon Whitehead, Deputy Director of the National Development Team, and Janice Robinson, Director of the Community Care Programme at the King's Fund, for their advisory role and to Alison Wertheimer for her skill and dedication to the major task of co-ordinating the contributions of our writers.

Thanks also to Giovanna Ceroni, Editor, Minuche Mazumdar, Design Manager, and Linda Moore for her administrative and word-processing support.

A special thank you to people with learning difficulties up and down the country who influence us day by day through their willingness to work with us and share their hopes and dreams for their futures.

Barbara McIntosh
Andrea Whittaker
Changing Days Project

Acknowledgements

Our grateful thanks go to the following people who wrote chapters or parts of chapters for this book, working under some pressure to produce material in the short time we had available.

Steve Beyer	Deputy Director, Welsh Centre for Learning Disabilities, Meridian Court, North Road, Cardiff CF4 3BL. Tel: 01222 691695
Paul Chapman	UNISON, 1 Mabledon Place, London WC1H 9AJ. Tel: 0171 388 2366
Denny Cruikshank	Barnet Healthcare, Colindale Hospital, Colindale Avenue, Colindale, London NW9 5HG. Tel: 0181 205 1777
Jackie Downer	13 Andrew Walk, John Ruskin Street, London SE17. Tel: 0171 252 5358
Kathryn Green	Wigan and Leigh College, Wigan Campus, PO Box 53, Parsons Walk, Wigan WN1 1RS. Tel: 01942 501501
Duncan Greig	7 Woodford Road, Walford, Herts. WD1 1PB
Joanna Hurry	7 West Street, Bishops Lydeard, Taunton, Somerset TA4 3AU. Tel: 01823 433848
Sharon Lytton	45 Cromwell Avenue, London N6 5HP. Tel: 0181 341 2006
Barbara McIntosh	King's Fund, 11–13 Cavendish Square, London, W1M OAN. Tel: 0171 307 2400
Kate Nash	Employers Forum on Disability, Nutmeg House, 60 Gainsford Street, London SE1 2NY. Tel: 0171 403 3020
Mandy Neville	Circles Network, Pamwell House, 160 Pennywell Road, Upper Easton, Bristol BS5 0TX. Tel: 0117 939 3917

Nicky Newberry	The Garden Flat, 33 Cadogen Road, Surbiton, Surrey KT6 4DJ. Tel: 0181 390 2382
Christine Paley	The Whitworth Centre, Noke Hill Road, Harold Hill, Romford RM3 7YA. Tel: 01708 773004
Tony Phillips	Creewood, Brewers End, Takeley, Essex CM22 6QH. Tel: 01279 871447
Richard Poxton	King's Fund, 11–13 Cavendish Square, London W1M 0AN. Tel: 0171 307 3400
Mark Reeves	Rho Delta, Merlin House, 122/126 Kilburn High Road, London NW6 4HY. Tel: 0171 372 3989
John Van Rooyen	Van Rooyen Design, 18 Ridge Road, London N8. Tel: 0181 348 2378
Lydia Sinclair	Scott-Moncrieff, Harbour and Sinclair, Signet House, 49–51 Farringdon Road, London EC1M 3JB. Tel: 0171 242 4114
Jean Taylor	Director, Mencap London Division, 115 Golden Lane, London EC1Y OTJ. Tel: 0171 454 0454
Simon Whitehead	NDT, St Peters Court, 8 Trumpet Street, Manchester M1 5LW. Tel: 0161 228 7055
Andrea Whittaker	King's Fund, 11–13 Cavendish Square, London W1M 0AN. Tel: 0171 307 2400
Mike Wilkinson	NACAB SSU, 65 Waterloo Road, Wolverhampton WV 4QU. Tel: 01939 270805
Jim Williams	Team Manager, L D Directorate, Olive Mount, Old Mill Lane, Liverpool L15 8LW. Tel: 0151 250 3000, ext. 255

We would also like to thank the following people who assisted in various ways.

Tom Noon	Rho Delta Consultants, Merlin House, 122/126 Kilburn High Road, London NW6 4HY. Tel: 0171 372 3989
Frances Presley,	SHARE Project, King's Fund, 11–13 Cavendish Square, London W1M 0AN. Tel: 0171 307 2400
Joan Smith	Hallmead Day Centre, Anton Crescent, off Collingwood Road, Sutton, Surrey. Tel: 0171 770 5000
Sarah Woodin	TSI, Ashleigh, Sunnyside, Todmorden, Lancs OL14 7AP. Tel: 01706 813555

Executive summary

The possibilities and opportunities for change exist at different levels and for different numbers of people. If all the pre-conditions are right at all levels, major change is possible to benefit the maximum number of people.

Change can take place at:

- the individual level;
- the service level;
- the strategic level.

At the individual level, better opportunities are more likely if:

- care management is in place and accessible for people with learning disabilities;
- key or named keyworkers are linked to people in existing services;
- person-centred planning processes are used;
- personal support is available for people in their different activities;
- there is access to advocacy for people unable to speak for themselves;
- inclusion is sought in everyday activities of employment, education and training, recreation and relationships;
- risks are taken with appropriate safeguards.

These opportunities will be possible for more people if at the service level:

- service managers have change management skills;
- ways are sought to include service users and carers in thinking about planning change;
- there is capacity (skill, time, money) for service developments, particularly in the fields of supported employment and supported living;
- access/inclusion is sought in local colleges, and other public amenities;
- attention is paid to staff development and training.

Substantial progress will be made for the most people, if at the strategic level:

- there is political commitment to change;

- there is strong leadership;
- collaborative relationships exist or are developed with major stakeholders: service users, carers, other commissioners, providers;
- a clear vision exists of what is desired, backed up by a commissioning strategy setting out the steps to achieve it;
- arrangements are made for transitional funding, devolved budgeting, and individualised purchasing;
- strong links are made with the community, particularly employers.

Easy-to-read summary

Introduction

This book has been put together in a way we hope will help anyone who wants to know what it says.

We hope that

- people with learning difficulties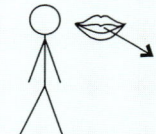

- parents/families

- staff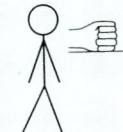

- managers

will all be able to read it and find new ideas and good ways of working.

We hope the pictures and symbols will be helpful. Most are quite straightforward, but the ones below might need some explanation.

help/support

needs

services

strengths

together

work/job

Our thanks particularly for help with this part of the book to: Jackie Downer, Independent self-advocacy consultant; Mark Drake, London Boroughs People First; John Sims, London Boroughs People First; Changing Days User Groups in Cambridge and Hackney.

Pictures and symbols taken from: *A Guide to Using Symbols*, Phoenix NHS Trust; *Rebus Glossary; Picture Communication Symbols*, Mayer-Johnson.

Chapter 1

From make-believe to the real world

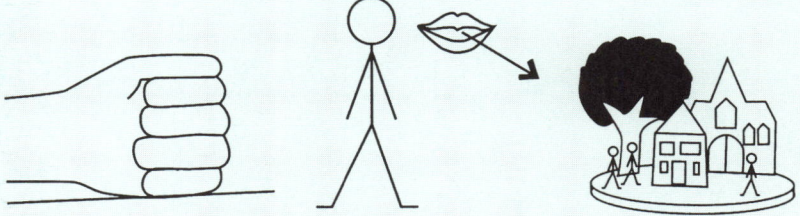

This book is about helping people with learning difficulties do more interesting things in their lives – get a job, go to college, do voluntary work, take up new hobbies.

At the moment, this is only happening for a few people with learning difficulties.

The book shows how services need to change to make this happen for everyone.

This is still a dream for many people because:

- people with learning difficulties don't know what is available

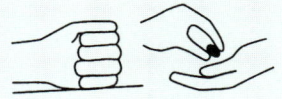

- services often don't listen to what people want

- services are still learning how to offer choices in the community

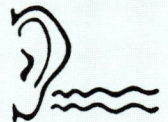

- services are still learning how to listen to parents and families and work with them.

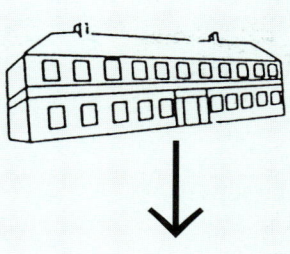

In the past, most people lived in hospitals or institutions. Now many people live in houses or hostels in the community. Some people live independently in their own house or flat.

But in the daytime, many people don't have any choice except to go to a day centre. Some day centres offer people a lot of different things to do at the centre and out in the community. But many people with learning difficulties find centres very boring places.

Also many people don't have anything to do at weekends.

For many people, their life looks like this:

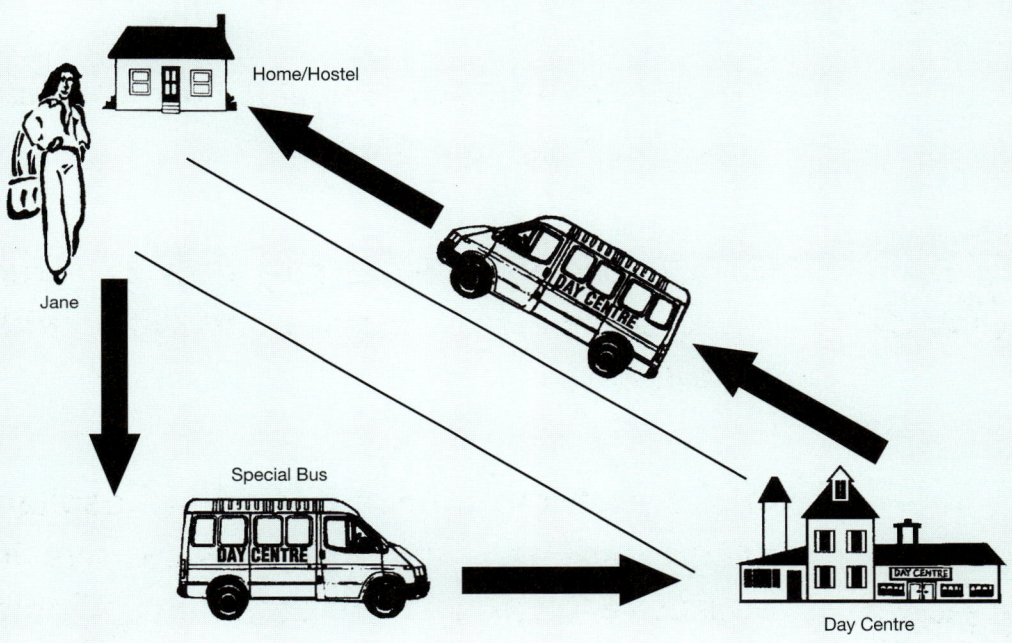

Home/Hostel

Jane

Special Bus

Day Centre

When what they would like to do looks like this:

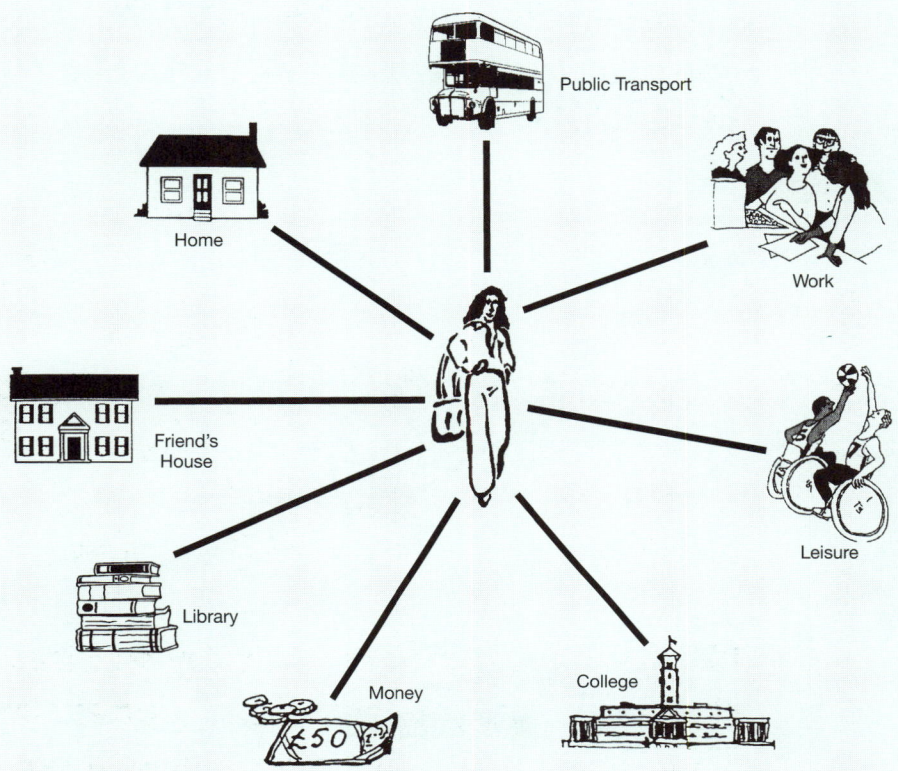

Public Transport

Home

Work

Friend's House

Leisure

Library

Money

College

There is a big job to be done. But if people with learning difficulties, their parents and families, and services work together, we can do it!

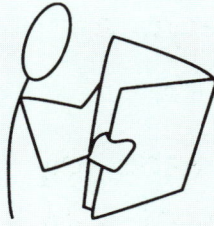

Read more
You can read more about services now and in the future on pages 1–5.

Chapter 2

Making big changes happen

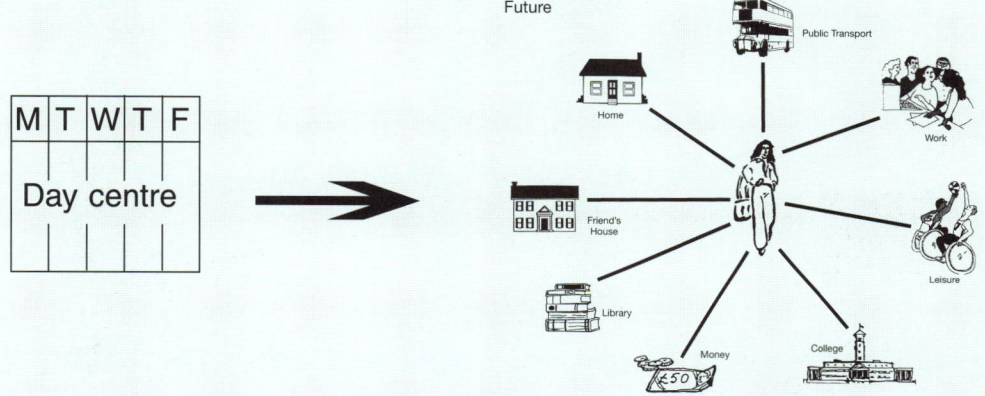

Many service workers want day services to change so that people have better lives. The Government is encouraging them to do this.

Good things are happening for a small number of people. For example, more people are getting jobs. But we need to make good things happen for everyone.

Services which have already made big changes are very different. Instead of going to a day centre every day, people go to different places during the week.

- Some people have a full-time job and go to clubs or sports centres or out on trips in the evenings and at weekends.

- Some people have a part-time job for two or three days and go to college on the other days.

- Some people do different things each day. For example:

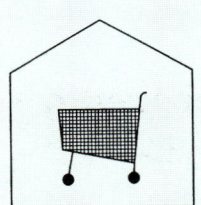

Two days – college

One day – a job or work experience

One day – at home washing, or cleaning, or learning to cook, or going shopping

One day – going swimming, to a drama class or doing voluntary work

Supported living

There are also some people who have never gone to a day centre because they don't need to.

They may have a job in the daytime and see their friends in the evenings and at weekends. Each morning they go straight from their home to college, or work or the leisure centre, just like their families and neighbours do.

Often they have someone to help them if they need it – a keyworker or a social worker or a landlady.

Most of the time they live independently – do what they want when they want to.

Changing services

Services are changing in different ways.

- *Making big changes quickly.* This means setting up different services over a short time – say two to three years.

- *Making big changes slowly.* This means setting up different services more slowly over a longer time.

Whichever way services decide to change, they must make sure that people with learning difficulties are not left with nothing to do or no way of seeing their friends.

Good ways to change services

- Everyone must work together – people with learning difficulties, parents, staff, managers and politicians.

- People with learning difficulties should be involved from the beginning.

- Managers and staff should:

  –   tell them what is happening

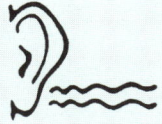

–   ask what they think
–   listen carefully to what they say
–   answer their questions.

Parents need to know that if their son or daughter is not going to a day centre they will be going to places where they can learn new skills and do things they want to do; and that there will be enough staff to support them properly.

Change can be frightening. But it can also be exciting when people work together to make good things happen.

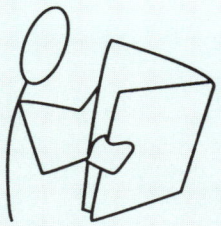

Read more
You can read more about changing services on pages 7–18.

Chapter 3

Partnerships for change

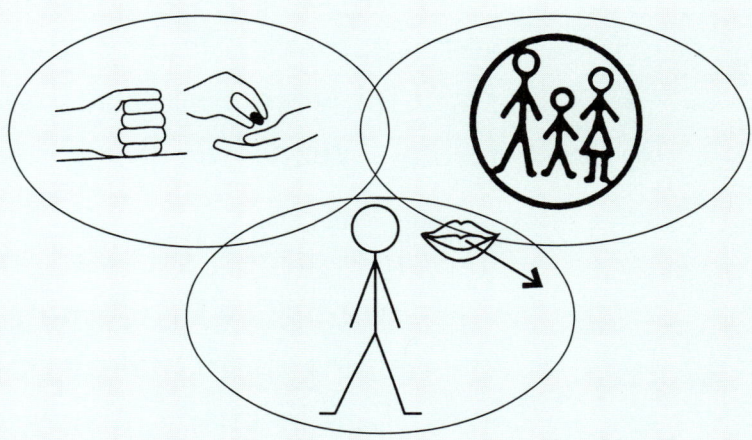

Services should work in partnership with people with learning difficulties, their parents and carers.

People with learning difficulties have needs and wishes about what they want to do with their lives.

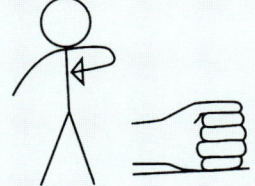

Parents and carers also have needs and wishes.

Some of these needs and wishes might be the same – some might be different.

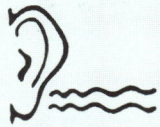

Services must listen to everyone and take action to make things happen.

Working in partnership with service users and their families should be the way services work every day. It is not just something for special meetings once or twice a year.

In some places, services are working well with people with learning difficulties and are helping them make good plans for their lives. But in many places this is still not happening.

In some places, services are working well with parents and carers. But in many places services are still not taking notice of things parents and carers worry about. For example:

- will new opportunities be available for everyone, or will some people get left out?

- will my son still be able to see the friends he has at the day centre?

- will my daughter lose her benefits if she gets a job?

Good ways in which managers can help

- Make sure all staff know how important it is to work in partnership with users and carers.

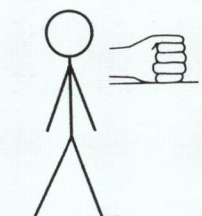

- Train staff so that they can communicate with all service users, including those who can't speak for themselves.

- Give people the chance to have self-advocacy and assertiveness training.

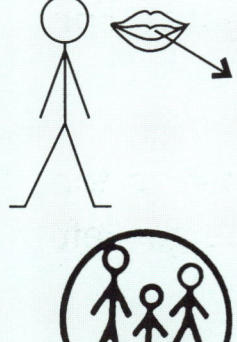

- Help users and carers take part in meetings easily. For example, provide transport, have summaries and tapes of meeting notes, have meetings at times and places that suit users and carers.

● Find out what skills users and carers have that could be used to help change services

● Help users and carers find out about other day services. For example, arrange visits, lend videos, invite speakers.

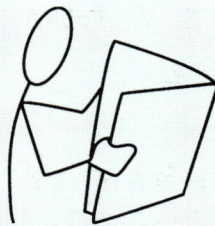

Read more
You can read more about partnerships with parents and carers on pages 19–23.

Chapter 4

Education

Education is very important to all people with learning difficulties. Everyone should have the chance to go to college after they leave school.

It is important that people get to know about colleges before they leave school. If they understand what college is and the courses and classes they can go to, they are more likely to enjoy it and do well.

You can go to classes that help you get a job.

You can go to classes to learn a new hobby, like photography or pottery.

You can go to classes to learn how to

speak up for yourself or to feel more confident about meeting new people.

Many people with learning difficulties now go to college for all or part of each week. Often they go to classes that are just for people with learning difficulties. They should also be able to go to classes with the other students. Sometimes this happens, but it should happen much more often.

What does this mean for managers and staff?

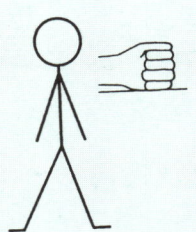

Managers and staff in social services must understand how important education is. They must understand that it can make it easier to get a job. It can give people more choice – more interesting and enjoyable things to do in the daytime, evenings and at weekends

Managers and staff in services need to work together with staff at schools, colleges and adult education centres.

Good ways of helping

- Give people the chance to try out different classes and courses. These are often called 'taster' sessions.

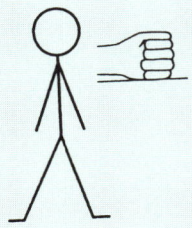

- Make sure there are staff in colleges who are there specially to help people with disabilities. For example, to help people find their way around the building or to help people decide what classes to do.

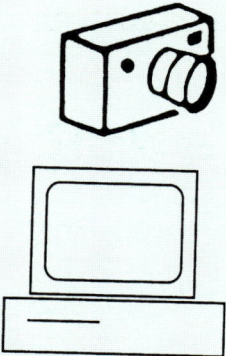

● For people who can't speak, build up a story of their life – their likes and dislikes, interests – using pictures, photographs, video, computers, to help them decide what they would like to do.

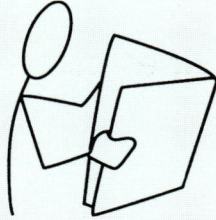

Read more
You can read more about education on pages 25–33.

Chapter 5

Supported employment

Having a job is very important. Many people with learning difficulties have not had the chance to get a job.

Organisations wanting to help people get jobs should:

- make sure they are real jobs with real wages
- give people the help they need to do the job well
- give people the chance to change their job if they want to
- help people with severe disabilities also to get jobs.

What does this mean for managers?

Train staff to be able to find jobs for people and find the right person for each job.

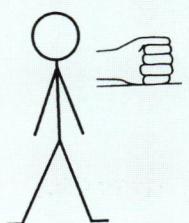

Change the way staff in day centres work so that they have time to find jobs for people.

Involve parents and families in developing job opportunities.

Ask people what sort of job they might like and give them a chance to try different jobs.

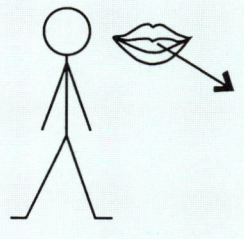

What does this mean for people with learning difficulties?

The most important thing is that you want to have a job.

Being a worker is very different from attending a day centre.

A working day is longer than a day at a day centre. At first it might be tiring. But you do interesting things, learn new skills and meet new people. You also earn money!

What does this mean for parents or carers?

Parents can help their son or daughter with suggestions about possible jobs. They can go with them to a job centre.

Parents may know about local employers who might have a job vacancy.

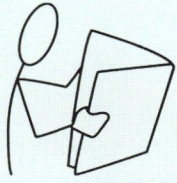

Read more
You can read more about supported employment on pages 35–47.

Chapter 6

Getting involved in your local community

This chapter is about helping people to become part of their local community: knowing their neighbours; using the supermarket; belonging to a sports club; going to the pub; worshipping in church; synagogue or temple.

It also means making new friends and having opportunities to help other people in the community – like working as a volunteer at a children's playgroup or doing shopping for older people.

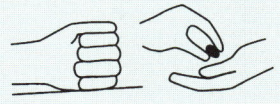

Many staff would like to help people do these things, but are stopped by the way services are organised. They say:

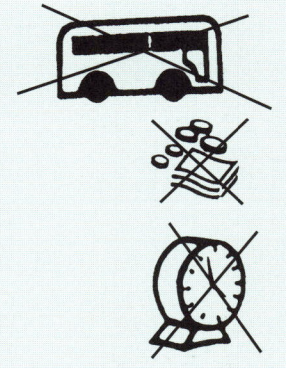

there's no transport

not enough money

it would be too risky

not enough time.

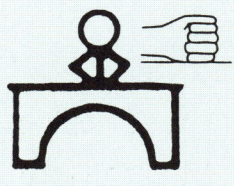

What does this mean for managers and staff?

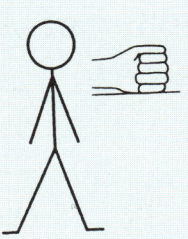

● Everyone in services – from top to bottom – need to believe that people should be part of their community. That making links and making friends in the community is important for everyone.

● Services need to let more staff work in this way. This might mean changing some of the job descriptions of staff.

- Services need to employ staff who know about the community.

- Managers need to support staff to work in different ways.

- Services must put in long-term funding for this work – not just funding for two or three years.

What does this mean for parents and carers?

Parents and other family members can be the most important people in helping someone get to know more people outside their own family circle.

But some parents may need help to let their sons and daughters do more things. They might be scared they would get hurt. They might not think they are able to do things on their own.

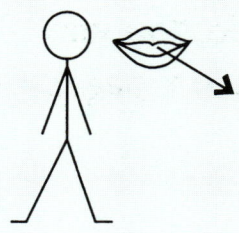

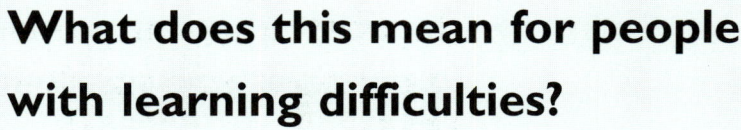

What does this mean for people with learning difficulties?

Many more people with learning difficulties are now getting out and about in the community, taking part in a wide range of activities at colleges and leisure centres and doing voluntary work.

But some people who have been going to a day centre for many years may be afraid to try new things. They may not feel confident about going to new places or meeting new people.

Good ways of helping

- People who used to go to a day centre can help their friends, encouraging them and going with them to try something new.

- Have a circle of support. This starts with people you know well – it might be family, friends or staff. Other people gradually join your circle to help you do what you want in your life. You can read about someone's circle on pages 55–56.

- Have a paid worker to help people start making links with people and places in the community.

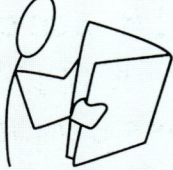

Read more
You can read more about people making links in the community on pages 49–59.

Chapter 7

Planning for individuals

Every person with learning difficulties should have the opportunity to make a life plan. Although the help of family, friends and staff will be important, the person should always be at the centre of the plan.

This chapter is about helping people with learning difficulties plan what they want to do in their lives.

It is important that a person has a plan for their life because:

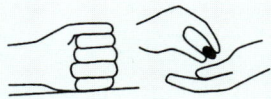

- it helps to make sure people get a chance to make changes in their lives

- it is a way of helping people with little or no speech make their wishes known

- it is a way of making sure services know what each person wants.

Good ways of helping people plan

- Start by asking the person what they want to do – what their hopes and dreams are.

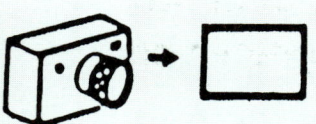

- If a person can't speak, use pictures, photos, video, computers – make up a life story book.

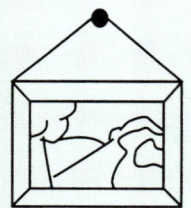

- Ask people who know that person well – relatives, friends, neighbours, support workers.

● Find out what the person does well.

● Find out what the person needs help with.

● Agree some goals or aims for the person.

● Choose some aims that are easy to achieve quickly. For example, Tom wants to learn to choose what clothes to wear when he gets up each morning. Other aims will be more difficult and take a long time. For example, Mary wants to live in a flat with a friend. Achieving some of the easier aims will help people keep working together on the more difficult aims.

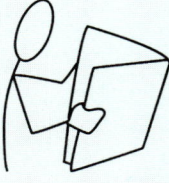

Read more
You can read more about planning for individuals on pages 61–66.

Chapter 8

Making it happen for people with severe disabilities

Every person with learning difficulties should have the chance to live in the community, including people with very severe disabilities.

These are often people who can't speak, walk or do anything for themselves.

They can also be:

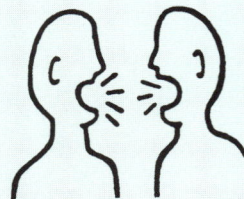

- people who get angry a lot
- people who injure themselves
- people who sometimes attack other people.

35

We need to understand why a person is behaving like this.

They might be frustrated because they can't say how they feel, for example angry, bored or rejected. They find it's the only way to get what they want.

Good ways of helping

Give people chances to learn a better way by being in ordinary places in the community, watching other people.

Take lots of time to get to know the person very well.

The person and their support worker need to trust each other and get on well together. This takes time.

What does this mean for managers and staff?

It can be difficult to help these people. Managers need to find ways of giving staff more time and more resources.

Staff should have special training to learn new ways of helping. Users and families need a lot of support to try different ways of helping.

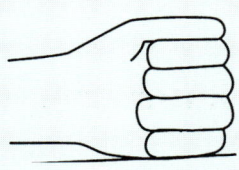

But when people start to live as they would choose and trust supporters to be helping – not just controlling their lives – their problems often get much less or disappear altogether.

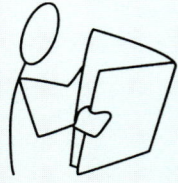

Read more
You can read more about helping people with severe disabilities on pages 67–74.

37

Chapter 9

Black and minority issues

It is very important that services look after the needs of people with learning difficulties from Black and minority communities.

As people are offered more choice of activities in different places in the community, services must remember to include the needs of people from different races and different cultures.

Black people with learning difficulties may find it particularly difficult to get a job. They will need extra support from services.

Good ways managers can help

Find out where Black and minority people are living in your local area.

Ask people from Black and minority groups what they want to do in their lives.

Ask people from Black and minority groups what are the best ways of helping them.

Provide help for people to come to meetings about services. For example, by paying for travel and childcare costs.

Provide training for staff on race and disability awareness.

People First have written a charter of rights for people with learning difficulties from Black and minority groups. This is what it says.

I HAVE THE RIGHT...

To be treated the same as everybody else

To have support

To speak for myself (in my own language)

To have a relationship

To be listened to

To choose my keyworker and my social worker

To practice my religion

To learn about my culture and my history

To learn about getting a job and money

To wear the clothes I want

To have services that are sensitive to my culture

To be treated as an individual

To make my own choices

To have information that I understand.

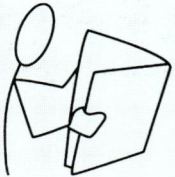

Read more
You can read more about services for people from Black and minority groups on pages 75–80.

41

Chapter 10

Staff development

Many of the best ideas about changing day services have come from managers and staff in day centres. They get to know people who come to the centres very well and have many skills to help people.

Some staff want to change the way they work and will find it easy.

Other staff may find it difficult. For example, in the community they might be working more on their own. It will feel different to working all day in the day centre with other of staff.

43

What does this mean for managers?

Managers will need to:

- help staff feel good about changes in the services

- make sure to use skills staff already have

- provide training for staff to learn new skills

- encourage staff to think of new ways to help people

- involve staff in deciding how to improve the service.

Managers also need to take time to look at their own needs and what changing the service will mean for them. For example, will they need to work differently with their staff?

Good ways to help

Organise training events where users and

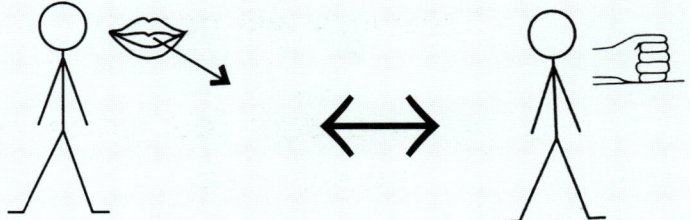

staff can learn together. Involve users in helping to train staff.

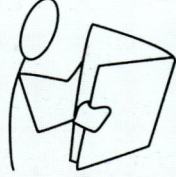

Read more
You can read more about helping staff on pages 81–86.

45

Chapter 11

Joint commissioning day services

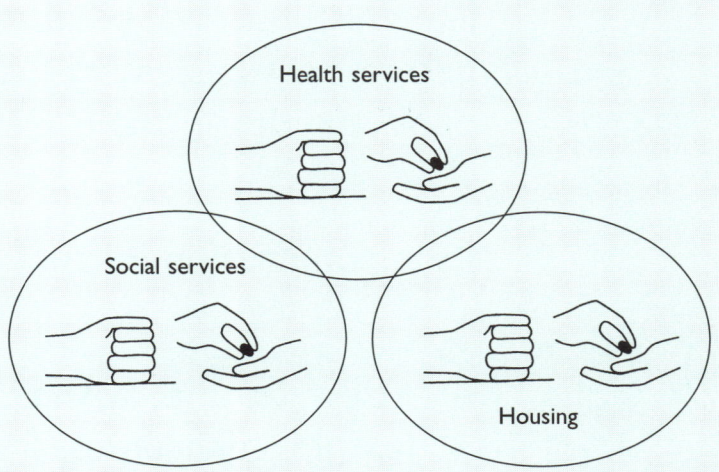

Public services are usually provided by large departments or agencies, for example: health services, social services, education, housing and employment.

Joint commissioning is about two or more of these departments working closely together to create services for people.

Often it is health and social services working together, but it can be other departments like education and housing as well.

When the big departments work together like this, it is hoped that people will get better services, more choice and more opportunities in their lives.

Joint commissioners should:

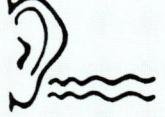

- listen to the wishes of people with learning difficulties, find out how they want to spend their days

- agree together how to make this happen

- choose people to run the services who will provide the best services

- keep checking that these people are doing what they said they would do.

Good ways of helping

Find out who your local joint commissioners are.

Ask to meet them to talk about your lives and how services can help. Invite the joint commissioners to a meeting of your day centre committee.

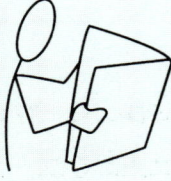

Read more
You can read more about joint commissioning on pages 87–92.

Chapter 12

Financing changing day services

People who run services have to plan very carefully how new or different services are going to be paid for. They have to work out a budget for how the money is going to be used.

Some of the questions they will ask themselves are:

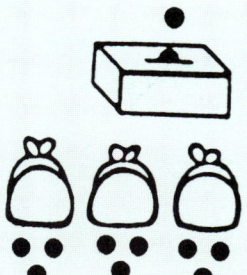

- Will the different service:

  save money?

  cost more?

- Will the money be enough to get a good service?

- How can we make sure we pay good salaries to staff?

- How much will we need to pay to use different buildings?

- Could we get more money? For example, by applying for new grants?

- Could we use the money we have in a different way? For example: less money on buildings and more money to employ more staff?

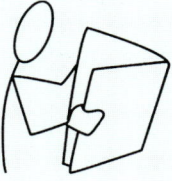

Read more
You can read more about finance on pages 93–97.

Getting around: creating an accessible environment

Most people go from place to place many times a day without thinking – from home to work, from work to the shops, from home to the library, to school or the sports centre.

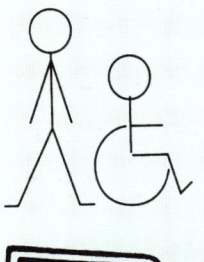

Many people with learning difficulties are not used to doing this. They are picked up from home or hostel in the morning in a special bus, spend the day in the day centre and are taken home again by the special bus in the afternoon.

As people spend more time in the community, they will go to a number of different sorts of buildings and other places like parks, swimming pools and shopping centres.

Some people will need help to do this.

Finding your way round the community

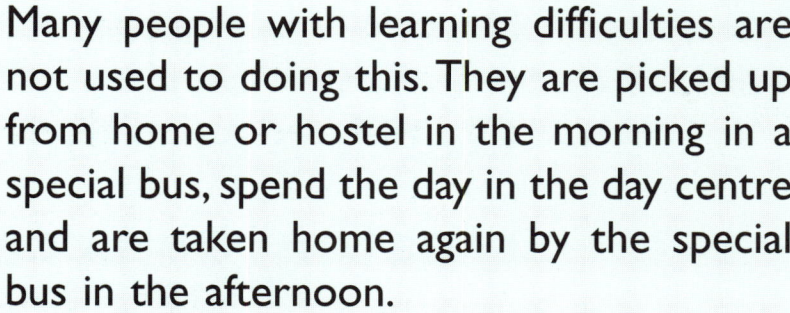

Most of us use signs like street names and place names to help find our way around. We also use landmarks like a church, a fast-food restaurant, or a phone box, for example. These are particularly helpful for people who can't read.

It could be a good idea to choose landmarks which are about a person's particular interest. For example: clothes shops, music shops or restaurants.

The person might need to go with someone else a number of times in order to get to know the route well.

Finding your way round a building

The sorts of questions you need to ask to help people find their way round a building are:

- Is it easy to tell which is the front door of this building?

- How do the lifts operate?

- Is it easy to tell which toilets are for men and which for women?

- Can a person in a wheelchair get in and around this building?

If the building is not easy use, staff and people with learning difficulties could work with the owners or managers of the building to improve things. Improvements will help everyone – not just people with learning difficulties!

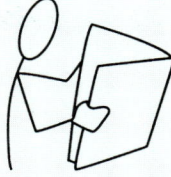

Read more
You can read more about getting around on pages 99–102.

56

Chapter 14

Transport

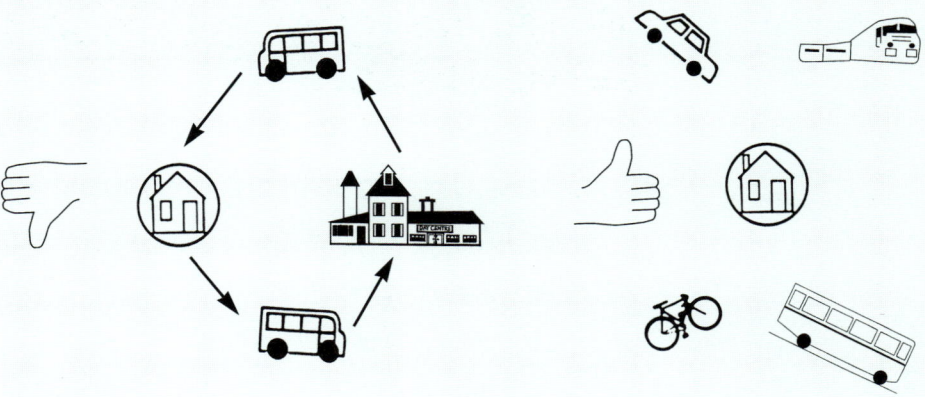

If people with learning difficulties can't get from place to place, they will not be able to take part in community activities. It is very important that services organise different ways of getting people to and from places.

At present, many people only have one choice – a 'there and back again' ride in a special bus from their home to a day centre.

Some of the good things that are happening are:

- a day centre organising its own pick-up service using day centre staff as drivers

- transport planning groups set up, involving users, carers and bus company staff

- more travel training to help people get where they need to go. For example: to work, the swimming pool, the shops

- helping people go to a place straight from home, instead of having to go to the day centre first.

What does this mean for managers and staff?

Transport needs should be a part of every person's individual plan to make sure they can take part in activities outside the centre.

Different ways of getting from place to place should be available. For example: sharing a taxi, using volunteer drivers, learning to ride a bicycle.

People should be encouraged to think of new and different ideas.

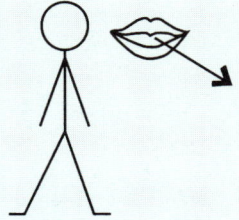

What does this mean for people with learning difficulties?

Many people with learning difficulties are used to being picked up and dropped off at the same time every day by the special bus.

Some people might be nervous about travelling in a different way. They will need encouragement and support until they are happy about the new transport.

What does this mean for parents and carers?

Parents and carers may be worried about the safety of their son or daughter using different transport. They might also be unhappy about someone having travel training.

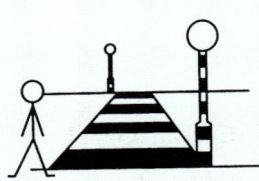

Parents need to know that their son or daughter will be safe doing these new things.

Some parents might like to join a working group to help plan different ways of organising transport.

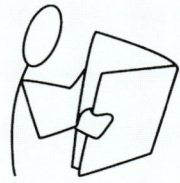

> **Read more**
> You can read more about transport on pages 103–108.

Chapter 15

Legal issues

 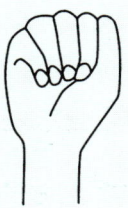 

People with learning difficulties have a right to community care services, including day services.

There are laws about how services should be provided.

The Government also sends information and advice to people who run services.

There are four important Acts – or sets of laws – which are about services for people with disabilities:

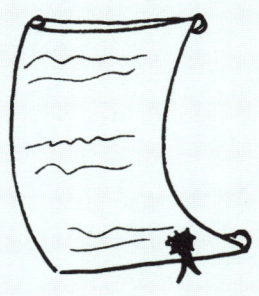

- National Assistance Act 1948

- Chronically Sick and Disabled Persons Act 1970

- Disabled Persons (Services Consultation and Representation) Act 1986

- National Health Service and Community Care Act 1990.

These Acts say many different things about what services should do to help people.

Some of them are about how services should work. For example:

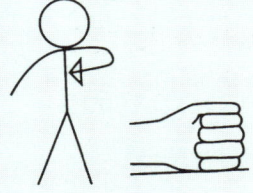

- find out where disabled people are and what they need;

- tell disabled people about services that are available.

Some of them are about different areas of people's lives. For example:

- practical help at home

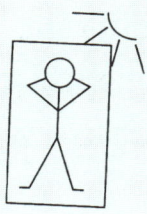

- leisure activities

- holidays

- education

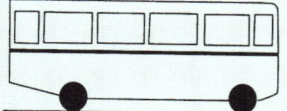

- transport

- employment.

Every person with learning difficulties is entitled to an assessment – to find out what they need to improve their life.

You can read more about community care and assessments in People First's book, Oi, It's My Assessment'.

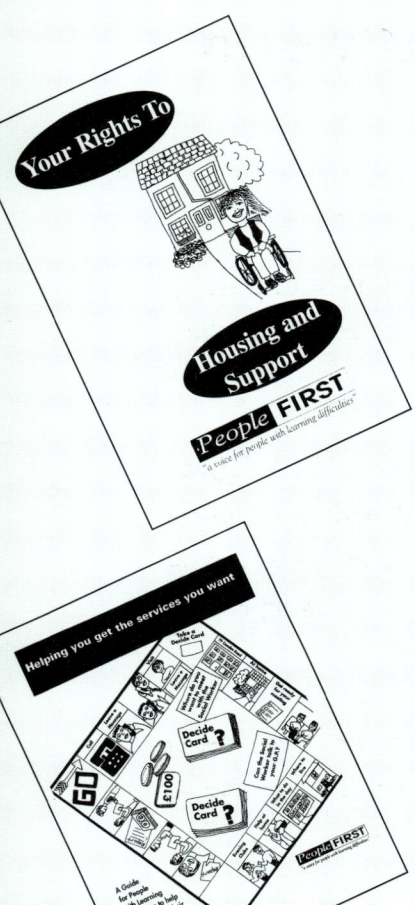

Laws and rights can be very difficult to understand. People First has published the following books to help people with learning difficulties:

Oi, It's My Assessment. People First, London Boroughs, London.

Helping You Get the Services You Want. People First, London Boroughs, London.

Your Rights to Housing and Support. Two books and a tape. People First, London Boroughs, London.

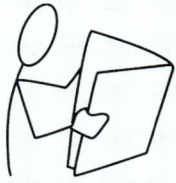

Read more
You can read more about legal issues and laws on pages 109–117.

Chapter 1

From make-believe to the real world

We are on a journey: from the artificial world we have created for people with learning disabilities towards the real world where we dream of supporting them in ordinary lives in inclusive communities.

It is still a dream, because we are only just learning what it takes to think beyond traditional approaches to 'service providing': to think ourselves past notions of special buildings, activities organised and often provided separately from the local community, delivered in ways that effectively disempower people and prevent them taking control over their own lives.

We are only just learning how to work with people as equals and partners; how best to enable people to develop new skills in the places where they are needed – at home, at work, in the community; and how best to support people to develop a lifestyle of their own, unencumbered by our own and society's prejudices and fears.

Where are we coming from?

The history of services for people with learning disabilities is generally full of good intentions. The Victorians recognised the need to provide support and education for some vulnerable people – though they did this by creating hospitals which were completely separate, segregated and supposedly risk-free. Later, when there were fears that people with genetic abnormalities might contaminate the gene pool, these hospitals became places of containment and control.

Eventually it was recognised that people were living in degrading and inhuman circumstances which denied their human rights. The process of running down and closing hospitals began, only to be replaced by new hostels and day centres which perpetuated segregation.

As the emphasis shifted to 'community care', parents were encouraged to keep their sons and daughters at home, but often on the understanding that 'care' would be provided in day centres five days a week. Occupation in these centres was initially based on simulated work and latterly on the idea of learning through 'social education'.

The human rights movement triggered widespread recognition of the importance of human values. The 'Ordinary Life' initiative, Wolfensberger's Social Role Valorisation (SRV) training and O'Brien's 'Framework for Service Accomplishments' have all had a major impact on the ways in which services are organised and delivered. Current government policy too emphasises person-centred, needs-led approaches.

Where are we now?

Despite this, the lifestyles of most people with learning disabilities are still largely dictated by services. Where they live, what they do, who they live with, where they go and who supports them are all determined by paid 'specialist' services. There is talk of 'individualising' services, but all too often this means people living in smaller groups but still segregated and still spending their days with other people with learning disabilities. It is just another version of the 'make-believe' world.

A small but growing number of people with learning disabilities are by-passing traditional day services completely. Supported living, based on individualised lifestyle planning, is enabling some individuals to pursue daytime activities of their choice in a truly integrated fashion and with whatever specialist help they need. Although supported living extends beyond 'day services', its individualised and holistic approach avoids the development of new service models and the artificial separation of 'residential' and 'day' services.

Day services for people with learning disabilities in the UK are still mostly about containment and occupation. In some areas, social education centres have been replaced by 'resource centres', combining a mixture of in-house activities with some excursions into the community. However, the commitment to providing weekday respite for many parents, the difficulties of developing individual programmes for large numbers of people and limited staffing mean that people still spend a great deal of time in centres, poorly occupied, and only going out in groups or to special segregated classes.

If you spend time with people with learning disabilities in traditional services it soon becomes apparent that they aspire towards participation and inclusion in the real world with a home of their own, friends and a job. But for many like Jane (see below), what they want in life and what their life is actually like are very different.

Present

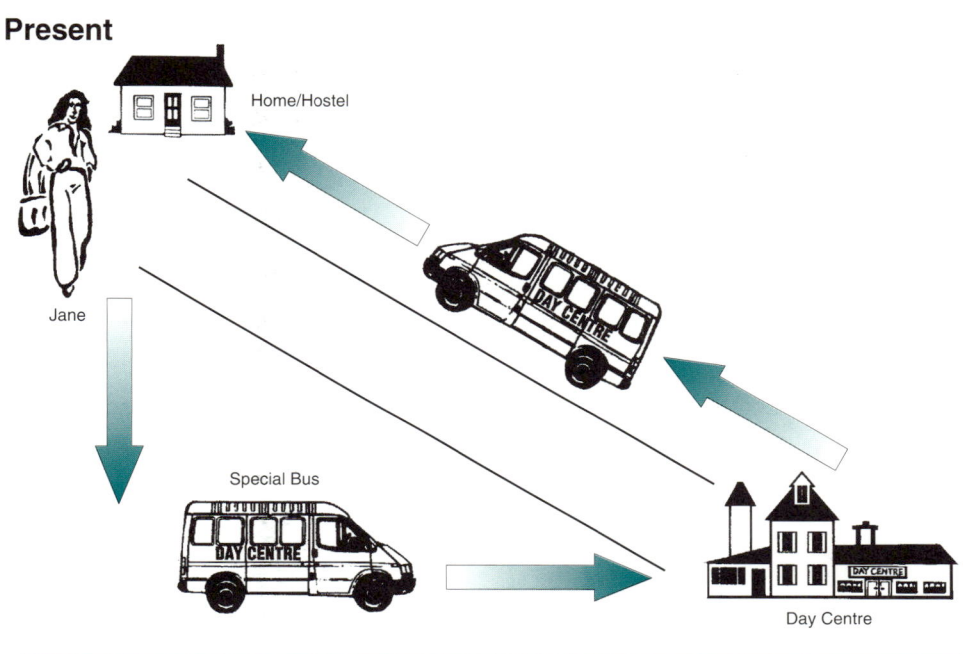

Future

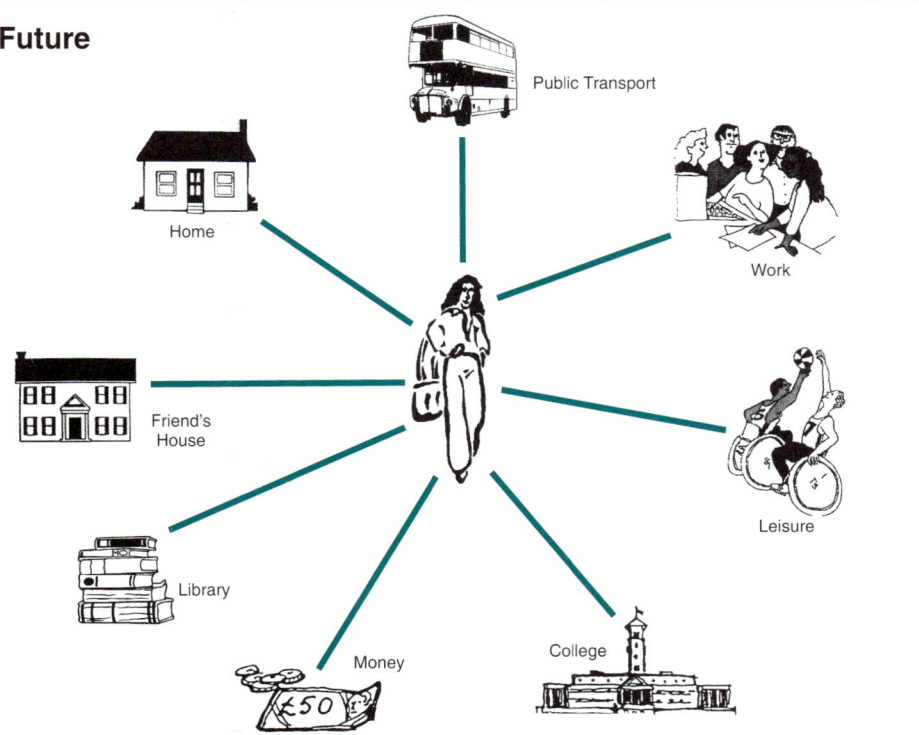

People with learning disabilities are now speaking for themselves and their message is clear: *it is their life and they want some major changes.* Most importantly, they want others to listen to them and act on what they are saying.

Of course some people cannot communicate with words, but there is no reason to believe that their aspirations are any different. The challenge is to understand how they would like their life to be. Understanding someone's aspirations cannot be achieved by functional assessments or using checklists. It can only come about through sustained intense personal contact, friendship and understanding – and a willingness to make informed guesses but accept that we still get it wrong at times.

The way ahead

There is a long way to go on our journey, but for the first time we have a sense of where we are going. We are not going to create yet another pretend world, but a real world. In this real world we will identify the supports that individual people need to help them live a lifestyle they are comfortable with, a life which offers the same opportunities we all enjoy.

This is an immense challenge for services that have been based on the idea of providing rather than enabling. It means facing and managing substantial change to the whole infrastructure of services we have created over the years.

Signposts for Changing Days

This publication offers guidance to those considering or already engaged in changing the way they deliver day services to people with learning disabilities. It recognises that the task is far from easy and that change will be complex and time-consuming.

It is complex because it is not about substituting one 'model' of services for another. The replacement of large hospitals with small units based in domestic housing has shown the pitfalls in adopting that approach: the inadequacies of the new model have rapidly become apparent. Setting up a 'model' limits people's choices, replaces one institution with another and fails to address fundamental human rights issues.

We are not talking about a single new type of service but about helping individuals work out what kind of life they want and can lead, and supporting them to achieve that.

There is already considerable experience of doing this for some people. In many parts of the country individuals have got jobs through supported-employment agencies or are attending mainstream college courses. The difficulty is that not everyone knows about them. But even in those agencies which have attempted this for a few people, the challenge is how to do so for many people: how to bring about change strategically and on a large scale.

This design guidance seeks to provide information about how new opportunities have been created for people in employment, education, and in local communities. It looks at the processes of change, management and practice that services need to address; it advises on what is involved in getting to know people, planning new opportunities with them, creating the appropriate support and ensuring safeguards are in place. It identifies the special challenges facing services: responding to the needs and aspirations of people whose behaviour is challenging or who have multiple disabilities; responding to people's differing racial and cultural identities; purchasing and joint commissioning; and ensuring access to the services and amenities in the community that everyone uses. Not least it looks at the implications of providing continuing respite for some parents, while recognising that the core task is supporting individuals towards a better quality of life.

Moving away from service 'models' makes it impossible to describe what an ideal day service will look like. To a large extent it will be invisible. It will be about individual people helping other individuals to go about their daily lives. Quality will be defined by the nature of the processes, the relationships between people and the extent to which individual aspirations are being met. Changing Days is about how we move from our buildings-based, service-led model to an almost invisible needs-led approach that supports people in the real world of our communities.

Chapter 2

Evolution or revolution: tackling strategic change

The will to change?

Many individuals and organisations are already thinking about change in their day services and the Department of Health has encouraged social services departments and others to think about new and different approaches. The will to make changes is there, evidenced by the rapid expansion of local projects helping people with learning disabilities get jobs.

But most of these schemes are small, one-off initiatives. It has been much more difficult for organisations to develop systematic and strategic approaches to changing day services across a whole locality. The vision is often there – in statements about individualised programmes, jobs, supported leisure activities and access to mainstream further education. But the mechanics of shifting from the current infrastructure based on large day centres to realising the vision are missing.

What have we learned so far?

We do have some experience of attempts to bring about strategic changes systematically and we can learn from this.

Revolution

This involves total reprovision of one or more traditional centre-based services over a relatively short period of time (two-to-three years). It requires strong political commitment from elected members, exceptional project management skills and intensive attention not only to planning new services but to consulting and involving staff, services users and families. The main advantages of this approach are that it demonstrates a commitment to major redevelopment and change occurs relatively rapidly. The main disadvantage is that shortage of time can force a continuing reliance on service-led solutions for some users, albeit in smaller but still segregated buildings.

Evolution

This involves the gradual replacement of day-centre-based services by systematically developing alternatives so that traditional services gradually contract. The most successful examples of this approach have focused on developing employment opportunities on the basis that that is how most people would choose to spend their weekdays. Initiatives of this kind have included finding jobs for people in social firms and co-operatives, and securing individual work placements. The main disadvantage is the continuing reliance on centres for quite large numbers of people over many years because of the relatively slow pace of change.

By-passing day centres

Supported living can enable individuals to leave – or never enter – day centres. However, even where agencies have developed this approach, they usually also have considerable resources still tied up in traditional day and residential services.

What strategic issues need to be addressed?

Experience from hospital closures, more limited experience of large-scale change in day services and what we know about managing change generally, suggest that a number of key strategic issues need to be addressed.

Commitment to change

Local authorities have a lead role in day services for people with learning disabilities and a high level of commitment is required from politicians and senior managers if opportunities for change are to be exploited to the full. Change will be required in every area, including infrastructure, funding and staffing.

Top down and bottom up

Top-down strategies for changing day services, initiated by senior managers, will only work if other staff, service users and families are actively involved and encouraged to contribute their ideas about changing patterns of day services. Organisations which rely solely on 'instructions' from senior management are less likely to succeed in taking other stakeholders with them. Generating ownership of and participation in change from the bottom up are equally important. One school of thought says that progress will only be made by developing new opportunities outside existing services, while others believe that without the support of staff in existing services change will be impossible. The truth is that both are needed.

Recognising the effects of change

Most people find the idea of change threatening – even when the outcomes are likely to benefit them. Resistance to change may be expressed through negative or hostile attitudes and attempts to block new developments. The feelings need to be recognised and talked about. If managers fail to acknowledge these reactions, change is likely to be slower or less effective.

Accepting unpredictability and encouraging innovation

It may be impossible to predict what future day services will be like in the absence of a single 'service model' for all users. The resulting uncertainty may be difficult to live with and managers may be tempted to look for 'the' answer rather than living without all the answers. Be prepared to experiment, try things out, and if that does not seem right then try something different. Avoid penalising people if something does not work out (there is usually something to be learned from the attempt anyway).

Resourcing strategies

We know from hospital resettlement programmes that as one service contracts and the other develops, strategies for reducing the investments in one and reinvesting those resources in the other are essential. Skilled financial planning and short-term investment to pump-prime new services are needed to take account of the temporary overlap in costs and the funding of project management. It is essential to explore all funding possibilities for these short-term additional costs.

Maximising resource opportunities

At a time of tightening fiscal control and budgetary cuts, it is unclear whether developing new daytime opportunities will cost statutory authorities more than operating current services. However, an approach which uses community-based facilities offering work or education certainly has the chance of attracting wider funding than day centres. Employment initiatives may be able to secure funding from the European Social Fund, Training and Enterprise Councils (TECs), or the Department of Employment. Further and adult education is funded through the Further Education Funding Council (FEFC) and local education authorities respectively. Community development has many potential funding sources.

Stopping the flow

Hospitals could only be run down if new admissions were halted and alternatives developed for those people who would otherwise have been admitted for long-term care. One important strategy will be to create different futures for school-leavers and work with health authorities to develop alternatives to existing provision for people leaving hospital. Different arrangements may also be made for people living in residential care or in their own homes.

Acknowledging the respite element

Many parents have come to see day care from Monday to Friday as respite from caring for their son or daughter. Proposals to stop or modify this have become a political issue in many areas, sometimes resulting in plans for changing services being shelved. In the short-to-medium-term continued provision of respite will be necessary for a generation of parents who have become accustomed to this but even this can be provided in more imaginative ways (e.g. clubhouses). However, it should not be assumed that all existing carers require respite or that their views may not change: when a parent sees their son or daughter coming home happy and fulfilled from three days' positive and purposeful activity at work or college, they may decide that is preferable to full-time attendance at a centre.

Developing supported living

One of the biggest pressures on day services stems from the fact that most people with learning disabilities either live with parents or in some kind of residential unit. If a person has their own home, they have somewhere to be if they cannot or do not want to be anywhere else. They can choose their own lifestyle, including who they spend their time with. This does not require a day centre. What they might need is support in a job or in using recreational, leisure or educational facilities – or someone to assist them in pursuing a range of activities at home.

Working with families with children

Many families become progressively disempowered over the years and encouraged to believe that their children will always need separate specialist services. Their expectations about future possibilities become suppressed and while they almost invariably find services unsatisfactory, they nevertheless continue to rely on them. Supporting younger families and encouraging their child's inclusion in mainstream life – at school, at home and in the community – will help break this vicious circle. Families will have different and more positive expectations for their child's future in which a day centre will play no part.

Involving users and carers

Change is always most effective when those most directly affected – the stakeholders – participate in its planning and implementation. This requires openness about what is happening, and ensuring that users and carers have every opportunity to say what they think, to be listened to and have their questions answered. It will require an imaginative approach to communication and consultation. Real partnership will also mean that users and carers see changes taking place as a result of what they have had to say.

Addressing the needs of staff

Most people seek stability and security in their lives, including in their jobs, particularly at times of high unemployment. Change can be threatening and staff need to be fully involved and consulted. Training and support needs must be systematically and sensitively addressed as part of the change process. This not only matters to staff themselves. Their relationships with service users are central and the quality of those relationships should not be jeopardised by staff anxiety and uncertainty about their future.

Change will only be effective and on a wide scale if it is coherent and co-ordinated. This is the biggest challenge day services face: to find a coherent strategic approach which does not lose sight of the fact that it is ultimately about supporting individuals. Addressing the issues in this chapter would be a good way to start.

Involving trade unions

Securing the support of trade unions in implementing change in day services is crucial, and managers should ensure that contact is made with relevant union representatives at an early stage so they can be fully involved from the start.

Changing day services can potentially enhance the working lives of staff in those services, but it is important to remember that people's experience of change will not always have been positive, to say the least.

Older, more experienced staff in particular have already lived through a process in which changes in community care philosophy and practice have frequently been accompanied by explicit or implied criticism of existing services. (As Nietzsche said, 'To make ourselves heroes of the new, we must murder the past'.)

This does not only apply to staff working in large institutions for it is abundantly clear that institutional characteristics can be found in small community-based day units too. However justified some of those criticisms may have been, some would argue that 'Care in the Community' has meant a backward step in some services in recent years.

Many of the problems do, rather tediously, relate to funding. While money is not a universal panacea, many goals become unachievable without it. Staff may tend to assume that any proposal to relocate and reorient services is motivated primarily by cost-cutting factors. It may be helpful, therefore, to share budgetary forecasts with staff to assure them that any savings will be reinvested.

Most people want rewarding and fulfilling jobs, and a guarantee of continuing employment, together with the necessary training and managerial support to fulfil new roles, is the key to getting the full potential from human resources.

Managers should not assume that they have a completely free hand to redevelop services as they wish. The Transfer of Undertakings (Protection of Employment) Regulations (1981) have resulted in many test case precedents which have protected the pay and service conditions of staff post-reorganisation. Expert and specialist legal advice should be sought at an early stage, and you may find that the major trades union legal departments can provide helpful (and free!) background information.

Many people find change threatening, and if they feel vulnerable respond by trying to defend the status quo and protect existing services. The way in which changes are discussed and negotiated with staff will be crucial if those changes are to go forward with their support and commitment, rather than in the teeth of fierce opposition.

What this means for managers

Managing change involves: managing communication among and between individuals and groups of staff, service users and carers; managing the organisational context in which change occurs; and managing the transition from the past and into the future. The following checklist offers a starting-point for thinking about change management.

Checklist for managers

- ◆ Who are the stakeholders in your current day services?

- ◆ Who might the stakeholders need to be in a new pattern of services? Are there other people/groups you could usefully involve?

- ◆ What forums for communication will you need to establish to ensure that all stakeholders are kept informed and are able to contribute actively to the process of change?

- ◆ What forms of consultation and channels of communication will best suit each stakeholder group?

- ◆ What financial strategies will be needed to develop and sustain a less buildings-based service?

- ◆ What financial systems will be necessary to enable you to purchase flexible daytime opportunities based on individual needs and preferences?

- ◆ How will you fund the transition phase when new daytime services are operating in parallel with existing provision?

- ◆ How can you involve people such as employers, local community organisations and others outside day services so that daytime opportunities move from the periphery of ordinary community life and become embedded in it?

- ◆ What timescales for change are right for your organisation?

- ◆ What would be the pluses and minuses of opting for fast-track 'revolutionary' change or a more gradual 'evolutionary' approach?

Revolution: strategic change in Havering

Actually making changes is always more difficult than any guidelines suggest. No matter how much preparation there is, efforts to initiate and sustain change refuse to follow 'recipes' or neat successive stages. There are no magic formulae! What follows is a description of the experiences of one local authority: what did and did not go well; what worked and what could have been done better; and what we have learned about the process of change.

The process started with two days for staff, users and carers, facilitated by an external consultant. Although this successfully highlighted the problems of an over-institutionalised service and produced a vision for the future, it also identified differing standpoints among the stakeholders and opened up some deep-seated anxieties about the future.

The importance of stakeholders

Every user, carer and staff member was a stakeholder and the degree to which they were involved was a key factor in determining the outcomes of the change process. Everyone had the opportunity to shape the future service – or to impede change.

Each person had a different stake in the service so interests frequently collided. What was in one person's interests was not necessarily in another's. Those charged with steering the whole change process had to be aware of when to accommodate and when to refuse to compromise. They also had to be able to work with conflict and not feel threatened by it.

Steering the change

Some people will always find reasons for delaying changes (especially in bureaucratic organisations), so it is important to sustain the momentum. A steering group of four key people helped keep things going, and project groups charged with working on specific issues such as assessment, transport and advocacy avoided cumbersome and protracted committee-led changes and also helped share the power base with more carers and users. The steering group's role was to keep people on task and ensure tight deadlines were met.

We found that change only really worked when we enlisted carers as co-workers. Within the framework of 'No change is not an option', we asked them to lead on particular tasks, using skills from their personal and professional lives and letting their decisions actively shape changes. It took us a long time to realise that we had been asking carers to trust us but we had not been prepared to trust them.

Windows of opportunity

Successful change is dependent on various systems working together at the right time. Our change process was helped by a political decision to sell the site of an adult training centre. This gave us a capital sum of £1.2 million to reinvest in new provision and the political support to do so.

We also had to enlist the support of others in the local authority – the directorate of finance, the land and property service, the borough solicitor, and the direct service organisations – as well as external agencies with a vested interest in change, including health services and the voluntary sector.

Leaders of change have to be able directly to influence all stakeholders and enlist their positive support. We found people were very willing to contribute to change using their relevant expertise, provided they had a clear briefing and understood the parameters of their role. The land and property service, for example, led on property searches, the borough treasurer did the necessary fine-tuning of the financial model and ensured that new budgets would balance, the direct service organisations helped the in-house team respond to the tender and carers led on transport.

Communication

Does anybody ever get this right? We tried hard but certainly did not always get it right. The groups of people we needed to communicate with were constantly changing and expanding, and our master circulation list was never up to date for more than a week or two. We felt it was important that everyone got to know about things at the same time to avoid rumours but our communication system constantly let us down.

Although we had a project management system, people tended to absorb information at different rates and would also interpret information differently according to their particular perspective. Not surprisingly people found it easier to take on board information which affected them directly.

We asked carers to vet information for jargon and general accessibility, we circulated a monthly project newsletter, and held regular networking meetings and consultations, but people still felt uninformed or misinformed at times.

Sustaining change

We found it essential to turn threats into potential opportunities and remain positive throughout. It was usually possible to find a way round, through or under difficulties, through a constant process of assessment and reassessment of the tasks in hand. The important thing was to be flexible enough to change our approach when something clearly was not working.

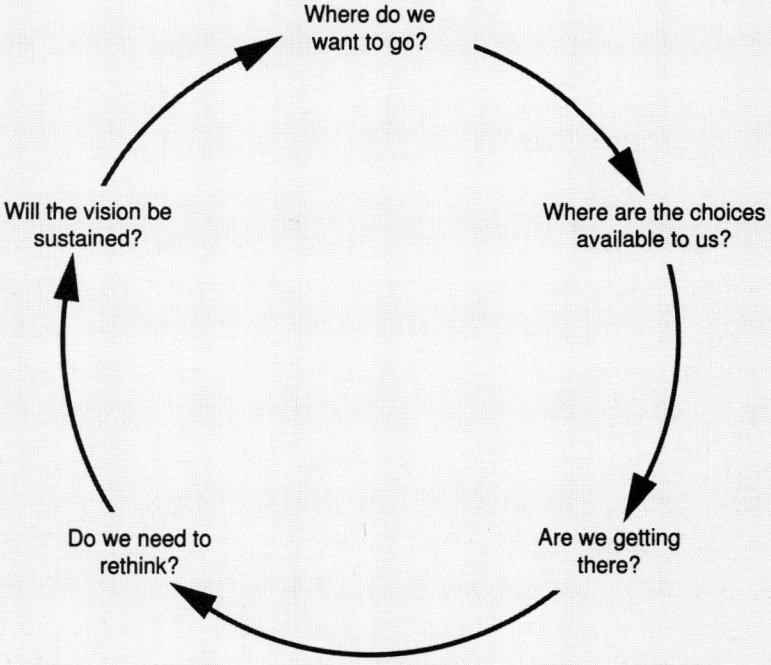

In this sense the strategy was never finalised but was subject to constant change. The route taken to deliver the vision needed to be flexible, goal-oriented and able to accommodate new directions.

Contact: Havering Social Services Department, The Whitworth Centre, Noak Hill Road, Harold Hill, Romford, Essex RM3 7YA. Tel: 01708 772222.

Evolutionary change in Clwyd

In the county of Clwyd, North Wales, (now the Unitary Authorities of Flintshire County, Conwy County Borough Council, Denbighshire County and Wrexham County Borough), there have been some real changes in day opportunities for people with learning disabilities over the last six years. Two key ingredients have been strong leadership from Graham Harper, a senior officer in the social services department, coupled with a clear vision of the future. Over the past six years, day services have moved from a buildings-based service relying on traditional day centres to the creation of individual employment opportunities. A work opportunities service (WOS) was set up, offering placements in open employment with individually tailored support by job coaches, and a number of small businesses were established to help people move from segregated day centres where many had spent their adult life.

In Flintshire, East Clwyd, where some 200 adults with learning disabilities are known to social services, 52 are now in supported employment doing ordinary jobs, backed by 13 job coaches, and another 50 are in small businesses set up by the WOS.

A noticeable characteristic of the WOS is its close relationship with employers. A well-developed partnership between Optical Fibres (a local industry) and the WOS has resulted in the establishment of several small businesses. One of these – Abbey Metal – was set up with capital from Abbey Metals. Optical Fibres staff have also demonstrated a real personal commitment to the company's involvement with people with learning disabilities. They are involved in a number of ways, including supporting people as co-workers and fundraising for new developments. Staff from Optical Fibres and WOS meet on a regular basis to discuss new ideas and plan new developments.

In the high street at Rhyl, a mountain bike shop called 'Tangible Dreams' was set up after several young men identified an interest in this area. They now work alongside bicycle engineers repairing, renovating and selling mountain bikes, and the shop is well known in the local community.

A number of ingredients have been central in helping Clwyd move from day centres to an employment-based service, including the following.

◆ The creation of working partnerships with local employers which recognise and take on board employers' perspectives, expectations and views about creating jobs.

◆ The role of job coaches in providing tailor-made support to individuals working in open employment.

◆ The recruitment of job coaches from a range of settings, including industry, the private sector and the commercial world, which has given diversity to the service. Their skills and knowledge combine with and complement those of the job coaches recruited from social services backgrounds.

◆ All staff in Clwyd social services having a commitment to moving away from day centres and creating opportunities in the community.

Benefits entitlements remain a problem for some people and can deter them from taking up a job. Most employers in Clwyd pay £15 a week to part-time workers and to compensate for this low wage, some provide taxis to and from work and others have set up funds which individual workers with learning disabilities can access to purchase gifts, holidays, etc.

Useful contacts

Co-options Ltd, Morfa Clwyd Business Centre, Marsh Road, Rhyl, Clwyd LL18 1LL. Tel: 01745 332300; fax: 01745 338008.

Work Opportunities Service, Charmely Lane, Shotton, Deeside, Clwyd CH5 1EB. Tel: 01244 814468.

Clwyd South Work Opportunities, 16 Gwenfro Buildings, Wrexham Technology Park, Wrexham LL13 7YP. Tel: 01978 290421; fax: 01978 355898.

References

Best, G. (1994), 'Managing in a changing world', *King's Fund Annual Report*.

Duck, D.J. (1993), 'Managing change: the act of balancing', *Harvard Business Review*, November/December.

Moss Kantor, R. (1989), *Can Giants Learn to Dance?* New York: Simon and Schuster.

Chapter 3

Partnerships for change

Vision and principles

Genuine partnership with and involvement of users and carers is critical if new daytime opportunities are to be truly person-centred and reflect the needs and aspirations of users, their families and friends.

Users and carers each have their own needs, and services should be seeking to help both achieve their desired lifestyle. Although users' needs and wishes should be paramount, it is important to recognise that carers also need support. (From 1996, carers will be legally entitled to ask the local authority for a separate assessment of their needs.)

User and carer consultation and participation can easily be superficial and tokenistic, however well intentioned services may be. It needs to be central to the whole change process. Self-advocacy is about more than just a weekly users' group at the day centre or a six-monthly meeting between carers' representatives and senior managers. This part of the design guidance focuses on users' and carers' participation in change. Other chapters discuss how both these key groups of stakeholders can play a full part in all aspects of day services.

The current scene...

... for users

Some people with learning disabilities are voting with their feet by opting out of traditional day services, even when no alternatives are offered. Others continue to spend their days in centres where there is a range of timetabled activities but no clear aims or defined outcomes for individuals.

The gap between what users are offered and what they are saying they want seem to occur, at least in part, because no one has asked them what they want. While the general trend in both the public and private sectors has been towards greater consumer consultation, services for people with learning disabilities have largely bucked the trend.

In some areas, attempts are being made to develop a more person-centred approach, helping individuals articulate their dreams and aspirations and devising ways of enabling these to be realised.

The introduction of the purchaser/provider divide has enabled some services to create less building-based solutions (e.g. renting out day centre premises and using the revenue to support people in a variety of community-based settings; or developing a service which starts from the user's home and by-passes a day centre all together).

... for carers

Carers have often been seen as opposed to any change: 'a force to be overcome rather than worked with'. Although this may sometimes be the case, too often carers' views have been neither acknowledged nor acted on. Their very real and justifiable concerns are often seen as overprotectiveness or interference rather than a genuine commitment to getting the best possible services for their son or daughter.

Although individual carers have their own particular agendas, certain issues crop up frequently:

- a higher quality, more varied service will only be available for part of the week;
- the new opportunities will only be accessible to those with the fewest support needs, leaving others with a deteriorating service;

- their son or daughter will lose touch with their friends if the service is more dispersed;
- the person will lose their benefit entitlement if they obtain (even part-time) paid employment;
- spending more time in the community will expose their son or daughter to unacceptable dangers and a hostile unaccepting community;
- they will only be asked to be involved when problems occur;
- new initiatives are not always sustained and if and when services do not deliver on promises carers will be left to pick up the pieces;
- day centre programmes are repetitive and could offer more variety, but carers lack information about possible alternatives.

Parents can also feel that change is happening too slowly. Younger parents whose sons and daughters have benefited from greater inclusion during childhood years are unlikely to want segregated day services.

Checklist for managers

Involving users in the change process

◆ What existing mechanisms does the service have for involving users, collectively and individually, in decision-making etc.?

◆ Are staff at all levels aware of the importance of user involvement in change and committed to making this happen?

◆ Do staff have the necessary skills to undertake consultation with users, particularly with people who have little or no verbal communication?

◆ Have you considered undertaking a survey to see whether the current service is providing what people want? How might this be done to ensure maximum possible participation?

◆ Could the organisation's training department offer assertiveness courses and other advocacy-related training for users?

◆ Are there users who could help other people to speak for themselves?

◆ Have you considered what supports people might need to take part in consultations about change?

◆ At the end of the day who really has the power to effect change?

Involving carers in the change process

◆ Is there a genuine commitment to involving carers in the process of change? Are you prepared not only to take their views on board but to act on those views where appropriate?

◆ Can you learn from the many examples of good practice in carer consultation which already exist in health and social services and do you know where to access information about this? You need to find what is right for you, but avoid reinventing the wheel!

◆ Do you have a range of consultation strategies which take account of diversity among carers in terms of their differing lifestyles, including cultural and ethnic differences?

◆ Have you thought about how you can harness the personal and professional knowledge and expertise of carers to assist you in implementing change? Carers can be a valuable resource.

◆ In addition to formal channels for consultation and communication, are managers and other staff easily available to carers wishing to talk more informally at other times?

◆ Can you help carers find out about possible alternatives to current day services (through provision of written information, arranging visits, lending videos, hiring speakers, etc.)?

Further reading

Although these publications will be helpful in thinking about how to involve users and carers specifically in change, they are also relevant to ongoing participation and consultation.

Beresford, P. and Croft, S. (1993), *Citizen Involvement, A practical guide for change.* British Association of Social Workers.

Croft, S. and Beresford, P. (1993), *Getting Involved. A practical manual.* Open Services Project, Tempo House, 15 Falcon Road, London SW11 2PJ.

Dawson, P. and Palmer, W. (1993), *Taking Self-Advocacy Seriously.* Nottingham: East Midlands Further Education Council.

Fiedler, B. and Twitchin, D. (1992), *Achieving User Participation. Planning services for people with severe physical and sensory disabilities.* Living Options in Practice Project Paper No. 3, London: King's Fund Centre.

Goss, S. and Miller, C. (1995), *From Margin to Mainstream. Developing user- and carer-centred community care.* York: Joseph Rowntree Foundation.

Lindow, L. and Morris, J. (1995), *Service User Involvement. Synthesis of findings and experience in the field of community care.* York: Joseph Rowntree Foundation.

People First (1992), *Oi! It's My Assessment. A guide to all you ever wanted to know about community care, your assessment and your care manager.* London: People First.

Robinson, J. and Yee, L. (1991), *Focus on Carers. A practical guide to planning and delivering community care services.* London: King's Fund.

Shearer, A. (ed.) (1991), *Who Calls the Shots?* London: King's Fund.

Chapter 4

Education

Vision and principles

The role of education is crucial in providing vocational and work-related training opportunities for people with learning disabilities.

Young people must be introduced to the idea of employment before leaving school so that transitional planning assumes that an individual's future will involve work and other community-based opportunities rather than a place in a segregated day centre.

Colleges should be seen as part of community provision, offering structured and individually tailored educational and training opportunities with appropriate support. The emphasis should be on progression: that is, devising a planned route through from one stage to another, with in-built preparation and transition arrangements. For some people this may mean moving to a higher level course.

Educational opportunities should be an integral part of the individual planning process and should have a clear purpose, whether related to employment, leisure or personal development.

Background

The role of education in day services has been discussed and debated for many years, since it was finally acknowledged that people with learning disabilities were 'educable' and capable of learning.

Almost 20 years ago, the National Development Group proposed that adult training centres (ATCs) should shift their focus away from contract work. They recommended the development of 'social education', encompassing not only literacy and numeracy but social and domestic skills, as well as work training or preparation. As a result, most ATCs became social education centres (SECs) and contract work largely stopped.

This shift to more education-oriented day provision coincided with the growth of services based on normalisation and O'Brien's Five Service Accomplishments, which placed considerable emphasis on enabling people to develop skills and competences. But unlike the National Development Group, which saw a continuing role for day centres, the Five Service Accomplishments envisaged people with learning disabilities using the same resources in the community as everyone else – including education facilities.

As a result, a substantial number of people with learning disabilities now use ordinary further and adult education provision. However, too often they remain segregated from other students. Not only do they attend 'special' classes, but general social and recreational facilities may be used separately from other students: breaks may be arranged 'when the canteen is less busy', for example. Despite this segregation, some colleges are including people in ordinary classes and in the everyday activities of the campus, by using support workers.

Further education generally has become more vocationally oriented and careful thought needs to be given to finding ways of including people with learning disabilities. Broader social education can also be provided in inclusive settings, such as adult education classes.

The current scene

Further education is now centrally funded through the Further Education Funding Council (FEFC). It places a high priority on provision for students with disabilities.

Although the FEFC guidelines emphasise progression and the attainment of national qualifications, colleges are also expected to offer equality of opportunity, individual learning agreements and support for anyone who has learning difficulties or finds it hard to access a course.

Most colleges have transition arrangements with local special schools. These may take the form of provision of link courses with the college, enabling pupils to take part in college life, sample different vocational areas and gain information about possible career choices. The courses can form the basis of individual assessment for the colleges which is crucial if the student moves on to college after leaving school.

The new code of practice for local education authorities formalises the transition process and should increase the flow of information between schools and colleges. Colleges will carry out a review process on exit from the college to aid transition to the next stage. Local education authorities provide daytime and evening non-vocational courses at further education colleges or in other community bases. These can provide opportunities for leisure and social and personal development.

What this means for managers

Managers of learning disability services should recognise that vocational provision can increase a person's employability and broaden their available choices for daytime activity. They need to ensure that their staff understand the importance of this.

Educational options should be considered as part of the individual planning process.

In order to access further education for service users, managers need to establish good working relationships with the co-ordinators for students with special needs and/or the learning support managers in local colleges.

Some individuals will require help which is outside the FEFC's remit: communication or work preparation, for example. However, it may be possible to set this up if the college and the learning disability service apply for joint funding (e.g. through European funding sources).

What this means for front-line staff

Front-line staff can play an important part in helping individuals to use further education facilities, including supporting them in college where appropriate.

They can also talk with individuals about how educational provision could increase their employment opportunities and inform them about local courses. This could be done in the context of keyworker systems or individual planning.

What this means for users

Individuals should be encouraged to think about how education could help them achieve their personal goals. People tend to be motivated to learn if learning is seen to have a clear purpose such as increasing their chances of getting a job.

What this means for carers

Families may feel that a change of direction, particularly one which involves the person being in a more integrated setting, is risky. They may also be concerned that the individual will 'fail' in some way.

It is important, therefore, to involve families in the individual planning process, particularly when there is a transition to further education. This could include visiting the college site their son or daughter will attend, and receiving information which includes positive images of people with learning disabilities moving through education and into employment.

Jane was attending a local day centre three days a week having completed a three-year college course. After initial assessment, guidance and work experience provided by the local Pathway Employment Service, Jane decided she would like a retail job. She started work in a large DIY store and had the support of a job trainer until she felt confident enough to manage on her own. She is now starting assessment for an NVQ in retailing and goes back to college one day a week to reinforce her on-the-job training. She is much more confident about communicating with other people and more mature in her outlook on life generally. Her parents, who were initially unsure about the placement, are now delighted with her progress.

Wigan and Leigh College

Wigan and Leigh College has been developing arrangements which centre on the individual student's progression through vocational courses to training and employment.

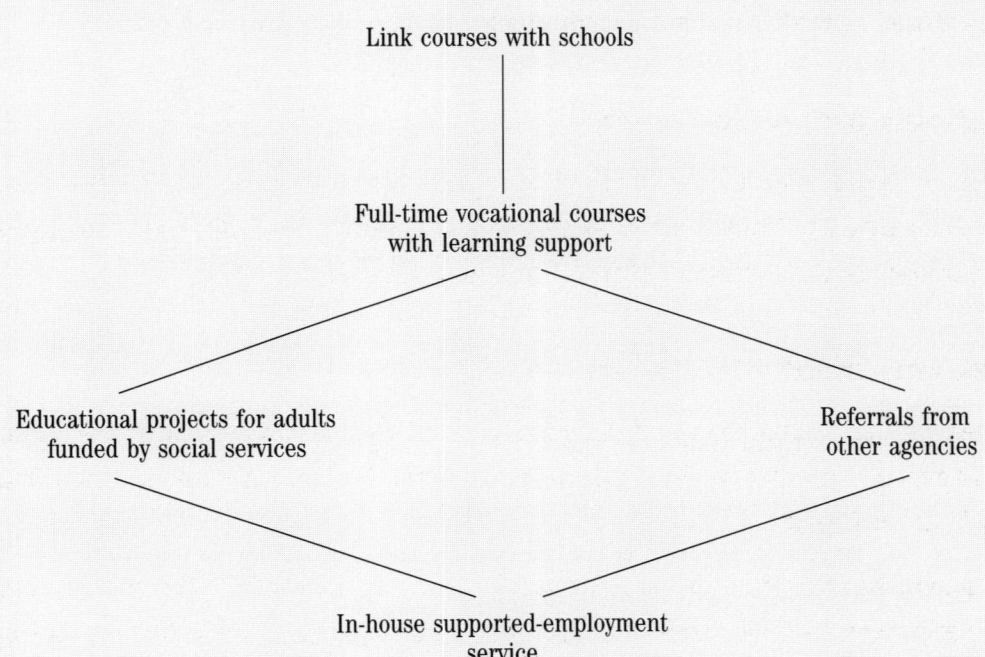

Link courses with schools

Full-time vocational courses with learning support

Educational projects for adults funded by social services

Referrals from other agencies

In-house supported-employment service

Link courses are established with local special schools, which aids the transition process for school-leavers. Students can then choose a full-time vocational course with learning support.

After completing the course, individuals can choose to use the college's supported-employment service rather than local day service provision. This offers training, work experience, and unpaid and paid employment, matching individual needs and preferences. Job trainers and support workers offer on-the-job support as required.

A joint college/social services project has also been developed, providing additional training for individuals before they are referred to the employment service, should this be necessary.

The Personhood and Citizenship Project*

In 1991 the Western District of the WEA (Workers Education Association) was funded by Avon health authority to provide day services for 25 people with learning disabilities who had recently moved from long-stay hospitals into NHS-supported accommodation. None was receiving community-based day services when the project began, either because they required a 'special needs' placement and 1:3 staff ratio and such places were unavailable, or because their severely challenging behaviour had led to exclusion from day services.

The Personhood and Citizenship Project was conceived and designed by Mandy Neville, the Western District's special needs tutor organiser. Informed by O'Brien's Five Accomplishments for Community Inclusion, the project offered adults with severe learning disabilities a combination of group courses and individualised learning opportunities in local community venues.

The project also provided ongoing training in inclusive education and positive non-aversive approaches to supporting people with challenging behaviour for WEA tutors, residential staff and others.

The Western District recruited a tutor-organiser and a team of development workers committed to person-centred education and with previous experience of working with people with learning disabilities.

Aims

◆ To offer a flexible alternative to the traditional day centre model . . . to enable people to live integrated lives within the mainstream of society while ensuring that appropriate, high-quality, well-structured support is available.

◆ To empower people to develop expanding networks and opportunities for citizenship leading towards independence within wide and varied social strata.

◆ To be guided and directed by the people who require its service through regular and consistent opportunities for consultation, negotiation and review within an appropriate accessible framework.

*This account is based on a chapter in Lauruol, J. et al. (1994), *Learning Together: An evaluation of WEA provision for adults with special needs across the English WEA districts*. Bristol: Norah Fry Research Centre.

Personal portfolios

Working closely with residential care staff, the team developed a personal portfolio with each student which reflected their likes and dislikes, interests and learning goals. The portfolio (based on Mariette Clare's (1990) work) took many forms, including picture catalogues, photos, sculptures and filofaxes. Most students had little or no speech so the workers used many non-verbal ways of sharing experiences to enable individuals to make choices. During the initial profiling stage, the team also began a variety of taster courses, offering new experiences to the students whose lives had hitherto been very restricted.

The programmes

The project provided morning, afternoon and evening courses in the local community, five days a week over three terms, plus an annual summer school (also open to anyone in the local community). Topics included: cookery, health and safety, dance, rights and choices, sculpture, drumming, landscape painting, drystone walling and how to run a café.

Tutors also held intensive one-to-one learning programmes with each student, working towards mutually agreed outcomes and with the aim of helping them lead ordinary lives in the wider community. Some students also chose volunteering, including helping at the local library, working on a farm and taking care of street flowers.

Courses were mainly held in local neighbourhood and community centres. For example: a cookery course was held in the parish hall of the church attended by one of the students whose friends were able to pop in and say hello. Venues were often shared: a music class shared a community centre with a mother-and-toddler group and a sculpture class shared premises with a young women's ballet class.

Advisory Group

The Group's meetings were attended by the students, the project's workers, residential care staff and volunteers from the local neighbourhoods, as well as the NHS Trust's managers and WEA District staff. Each gathering included an informal meal enabling people to socialise on an equal footing, followed by a more formal information-sharing session. Finally, everyone was invited to use a variety of media (paint, camcorders, photographs, etc.) to comment on previous courses and suggest possible future activities. Any problems arising were discussed informally between the parties concerned.

Each gathering was videoed and photographed. These records were used to inform future planning but also provided a striking statement about the breadth and imagination of the project. Many of the students had lived in hospitals, their lives documented only in medical or social services records, so the chance to give their views and be regularly photographed and videoed was significant. Along with the personal portfolios, these records reflect back powerful messages about valued selfhood.

Conclusions

The Personhood and Citizenship Project has some striking characteristics which set it apart from other institutional or community-based provision.

◆ Each student's individualised curriculum framework was developed collaboratively between the student, their residential carer and a WEA staff member. Although there were sometimes significant obstacles to using this approach it did empower very vulnerable and disabled individuals to make choices about learning.

◆ Most activities took place in fully integrated community settings, giving people the opportunity to move away from the segregation characteristic of day centres.

◆ Because the Personhood and Citizenship Project team were strongly committed to self-advocacy and respect for human dignity, there was a rare atmosphere of togetherness and equality among staff, students and the wider community.

◆ The project demonstrates that high-quality, person-centred learning opportunities can be provided with and for people with severe learning disabilities in the community, even where people's challenging behaviour has previously excluded them from day services.

There were also challenges. Integrating an innovative scheme of this kind with other services was not always easy. The project did not always sit easily alongside the residential services the students used. Neither did it fit comfortably into the WEA's usual pattern of adult education. Not surprisingly, the various staff groups had differing expectations of the project which sometimes led to conflict. However, schemes such as this cannot function in isolation. Effective relationships need to be developed with a whole range of other services and professionals. Staff time and other resources need to be committed to building good community networks.

Note: In 1995, the WEA ceased to operate the project. A new scheme, Choices for Learning, now operates on somewhat different lines, run by the Phoenix NHS Trust.

Contact: Choices for Learning, Greenway Centre, Doncaster Road, Southmead, Bristol BS10 5PY. Tel: 0117 987 7754.

References

Clare, M. (1990), *Developing Self-Advocacy Skills.* Further Education Unit/REPLAN.

Code of Practice: On the identification and assessment of special educational needs. London: HMSO.

Johnstone, D. (1995), *Further Opportunities: Learning difficulties and disabilities in further education.* London: Cassell.

National Development Team (1993), *A Way to Work: A report of an evaluation of the National Development Project 'Improving access to training and employment for school leavers with learning disabilities'.* National Development Team.

Sutcliffe, J. (1990), *Adults with Learning Difficulties: Education for choice and empowerment.* National Institute for Adult and Continuing Education.

Wertheimer, A. (1993), *Learning to Work Together: A report on the Studylink Project at Liverpool Community College (1990–1992).* SKILL (National Bureau for Students with Disabilities).

Wertheimer, A. (1995), *Getting Ready for Work. A work experience scheme for young people with multiple disabilities and significant support needs.* SKILL (National Bureau for Students with Disabilities).

Chapter 5

Supported employment

Vision and principles

Employment is one of the most important aspects of adult life, but people with learning disabilities have largely been denied the opportunity to enter the world of work. Having a job enables a person to participate actively in society, gives a structure and purpose to their day and is a marker of adult status.

Organisations wanting to develop new daytime opportunities for people with learning disabilities should be:

- *working towards inclusion in ordinary work settings;*
- *helping people find jobs which offer the same pay and terms and conditions as fellow employees doing comparable work;*
- *offering people the necessary support to function in the workplace;*
- *assisting those with severe and complex disabilities to find work and providing ongoing support where required.*

What is supported employment?

Supported employment is about placing individuals directly into real workplaces, using a tried and tested training technology and providing whatever ongoing support people need to hold down a job. A number of elements are essential to achieve the best outcomes for those in supported employment.

Assessment should aim to come up with a clear understanding of the individual's employment potential and expectations, a realistic picture of their support needs, and their skills, aptitudes, strengths and limitations. This part of the process is vital as it can greatly increase the chances of identifying a job which suits both potential employee and employer.

Job placement involves finding the right job for a particular person, ensuring that practical arrangements such as transport are in place, sorting out the benefits and ensuring these are understood by the individual and agreed with the benefits agency, and seeing that any necessary worksite adaptations are tackled. Job trainers also need to build up a good picture of the workplace, its culture and what opportunities for integration if offers.

Worksite training and advocacy include analysing the elements of the job the person will be doing, designing and implementing whatever training is needed and developing effective communication with co-workers and supervisory staff. When someone needs intensive training, the best approach is usually to 'fade' the assistance of the specialist job trainer until the person can work independently or as part of the ordinary work team. Some people may need continuing support for such things as personal care.

Ongoing monitoring involves ensuring that the worker's performance is maintained over time and that they remain happy in that job, doing any necessary retraining with them and keeping in touch with the employer.

Follow-up and retention are essential to ensure the person's continuing employment. They can be undertaken by the job trainer or by a co-worker at the job site. Improving the person's competence in doing their job and in a range of job-related areas (e.g. relationships with other workers) will reduce their dependence on others. People also need to be encouraged to develop their careers: a job is seldom for life these days!

The Employment Service uses the term 'supported employment' in relation to the Government-initiated Supported Employment Programme. We are including their definition, as it differs from that used in this document:

> *'The purpose of the Supported Employment Programme is to provide meaningful employment opportunities for people with severe disabilities who are registered under the Disabled Persons (Employment) Act 1944 and who, because of the severity of their disability and its effects on their productivity, are otherwise unlikely or unable to obtain or retain normal employment. Registration is only granted to people considered capable of making a substantial contribution to their own support. The Programme helps severely disabled people undertake the same kinds of work as non-disabled people apart from their lower output. They would be required to be capable of an output of between 30 and 80 per cent of a non-disabled worker's doing the same job. Work may be provided in purpose-built workshops for disabled people or in open employment in host firms.'*

The current scene

Some people with learning disabilities have already been through pre-work training and found jobs but they have tended to be the most able people. People with more severe disabilities and those whose behaviour challenges others have generally been excluded from these opportunities.

Supported employment has been developing in the UK since the late 1980s. Systematic Instruction, a training technology introduced into the UK by TSI Ltd (see p. 47), has played a significant role in the subsequent development of supported employment.

The number of supported-employment services increased from 24 to 79 between 1988 and 1991 (Lister *et al.*, 1992). Two-thirds of these were part of larger organisations, notably social services departments. Of the 1619 people with learning disabilities in work, 29 per cent were working full time but 45 per cent were employed for 16 hours or less a week. Supported-employment services continue to grow and the previous survey is currently being updated.

Those involved in developing supported employment currently face a number of challenges, including: the absence of a coherent funding strategy and a continuing reliance on social services funding; fears about losing benefits entitlements with some people either not taking up jobs or only accepting payment up to the therapeutic earnings level.

What this means for managers

Day service managers wanting to develop employment opportunities for service users will need to see that the necessary resources are available. Time and energy must be invested in working with everyone who has a stake in developing an employment service, including people with learning disabilities and their families and the staff who support them. Securing an initial shift in resources is essential but managers then need to make sure these resources are not diverted back into traditional services.

Staff will need new skills and knowledge to move successfully from a social services setting into the employment field, and managers need to make time for staff to make these changes and ensure that staff are not pulled back into the day centre – to cover for crises, for example.

People with learning disabilities must be at the centre of any new enterprise so that the employment service is user-centred and reflects individual needs. Families too must be involved from the start so that any concerns they may have can be heard and addressed. Families can be an important source of support for people entering employment.

Checklist for managers

◆ You will need to collect comprehensive information about each person seeking employment, including the kind of work they might like and any interests they might be able to pursue in a job (hobbies often spark off an idea for a job). Getting this information takes time – talking with the person, their families and others who know them – and managers need to find protected space for their staff to do this.

◆ Once you have an idea of the sort of job someone might like, the next step is to go out and look for an opening. Responding to advertised vacancies rarely works. Potential employers will need to be approached, and there is plenty of

---

written advice on how to go about this (e.g. McLoughlin *et al.*, 1987). Experience has shown that it will often be necessary to help employers create a job, by bringing together elements of existing jobs to form one job which the person can undertake successfully. Again, time must be allocated to allow staff to develop the skills of job finding and matching.

◆ It will be crucial to collect detailed information about the social and physical aspects of the workplace as well as about the job itself. This will involve discussions with employers and visits to the worksite.

◆ Good inter-agency planning about the practical arrangements can make an important contribution to successful job placement. The person may need training to get to and from the workplace on public transport, or other means such as mini-cabs may have to be organised. Dress, social behaviour and personal grooming may also need to be addressed. This involves talking with families and support staff in residential services so that arrangements are co-ordinated.

◆ Staff will need to learn techniques for teaching the person the job. Some people may learn a job relatively easily if they are shown what is involved and given some guidance. Others will need more detailed training. Systematic Instruction is the most commonly used method for this and managers need to allocate time and money for staff to develop the necessary skills.

◆ A supported-employment service must be able to respond to any problems arising after a person starts work. This may involve no more than a phone call but at other times may require a staff member to visit the workplace. The organisational task for managers is to ensure sufficient flexibility for staff to respond to employers' needs outside conventional day service hours.

◆ As with any worker, a job is not necessarily for life and managers need to ensure resources for career counselling and development. Staff will also need to continue working with families and other external supports to avoid job placements breaking down because necessary supports are lacking.

◆ Day service staff moving into employment-related work are likely to need additional support from management as they will be working more independently outside the centres.

What this means for front-line staff

As the previous section outlined, staff roles will have to change considerably. They will spend less time in centres and more time in workplaces, forging new links between people with learning disabilities and employers, etc.

Apart from acquiring specific skills, such as the use of Systematic Instruction, staff will have to reorient themselves from a 'care' setting and sensitise themselves to the concerns and working practices of employers.

Not everyone will either choose or indeed have the aptitude for this new type of work, but those that have made the move have often found it a highly rewarding experience.

What this means for people with learning disabilities

The person with learning disabilities is central to this whole endeavour and, if it is to succeed, they must want to work otherwise any placement will fail. If people are involved from the start they can set out on a career path and show that they can learn and develop into valuable employees.

Being a worker is very different from attending a day centre, and people will need to adjust to this and be prepared to develop a level of commitment and responsibility which may never have been required of them before. However, the rewards for them and those around them are potentially well worth the investment.

What this means for carers

Parents have a key role to play in supporting their son or daughter into work. They can help by supporting the person's choices and generally assisting with the adjustment to a different pattern of daily living.

In the initial stages, families can be invaluable informants about their child's interests, abilities and needs. They may also be able to contribute through their own contacts and knowledge of the local work scene. Parents are not only parents: they may also be managers, accountants, employers, canteen workers, supermarket workers and so on.

Supported employment offers families a new partnership, but also new risks. They need to be kept fully informed so that they can help their relative make sensible, and sometimes challenging, decisions.

What this means for people in the workplace

To help people into jobs and support their continuing employment, service providers need to develop good working relationships with employers. There has to be a real understanding of each other's needs, expectations and goals, and a genuine willingness to learn from and communicate with each other.

Supported-employment programmes need to develop an awareness of the needs and demands of employers. This may be as straightforward as presenting the employment initiative in language that employers can relate to (e.g. avoiding 'servicespeak') or as complex as creating a joint initiative with local employers.

An ideal way of bringing the various parties together is to set up a local forum or steering group of service providers, employers and other interested parties to develop viable local employment programmes.

Employers in the UK are becoming more aware of the benefits of employing a diverse workforce that successfully includes disabled people, and there are increasing cultural, social and economic pressures on them to do so.

Employers need to: understand the ways in which disabled people encounter discrimination in education, training and employment; develop new ways of attracting disabled applicants; and share information on disability issues among themselves.

The Disability Discrimination Bill currently going through Parliament is partly a reflection of increasing demands on employers to hire, retain and promote disabled employees, although the provisions of the Act are more wide-ranging and its enforceability is considered questionable in some quarters.

Traditional ways of getting more disabled people into work, including the quota system, have not been particularly effective, and experience in North America has shown that the most successful approaches consider the needs of a disabled person within the context of the employer's organisational and economic demands. In other words, people are not employed as an act of charity but on a sound economic basis, as part of the employer's business plan and with a realistic picture of any additional costs of employing a disabled worker.

Developing partnership can never start too soon. Invite local employers to participate in planning the supported-employment initiative, for example, get people from local businesses to do some training with day services staff. By creating a sense of shared responsibility, there is a better chance of creating working partnerships that effect real change.

The Employers' Forum on Disability

The Employers' Forum is the only national employers' organisation concerned exclusively with the employment and training of people with disabilities. A not-for-profit company, funded by its members, the Forum aims to improve the job prospects of disabled people by making it easier for employers to recruit, retain and develop disabled employees.

The Forum acts as a voice on disability issues at national policy-making level. It also works in association with The Prince of Wales' Advisory Group on Disability and in close association with Business in the Community.

The Forum was set up because employers lacked access to the information and assistance they needed to address the issue of disability in the workplace. By creating an information exchange, employers have been able to promote the business case for employing disabled people despite inadequate legislation and often fragmented service provision for disabled people. The Forum operates on the basis that better services for employers equals better services for people with disabilities.

The Forum seeks to improve the long-term job prospects of people with disabilities by:

◆ encouraging employers to extend their equal opportunities policies and activities to include disability;

◆ providing practical support and advice to any member wishing to improve their employment practices;

◆ working with Government, disabled people and voluntary agencies to improve policies relating to the training and employment prospects of disabled people;

◆ promoting attitudinal and environmental changes needed to enable disabled people to compete and flourish in the job market on equal terms.

Case histories

◆ The Central London Training and Enterprise Council has pioneered a new approach to supported employment for people with disabilities by joining forces with four supported-employment agencies. Twenty people received on-site training aimed at helping them secure permanent employment.

◆ The Bank of England have five trainees on the former Youth Training Scheme on two-to-six-week placements. Two had attended special schools.

◆ The National Autistic Society and the Employers' Forum recently launched a joint pilot scheme to provide people with autism with job opportunities, including an innovative alternative to the traditional job interview.

Contact: Employers' Forum on Disability, Nutmeg House, 60 Gainsford Street, London SE1 2NY. Tel: 0171 403 3020.

Social security and other money issues

There are several reasons why the social security system is often seen as an obstacle to developing new services.

Q. Aren't people receiving benefits restricted in the kinds of work or study they can undertake?

A. Existing employment initiatives have been tackling this and there are a range of work and benefit arrangements which can be used to meet the varying needs of individuals.

Q. Doesn't the complexity of the social security system and the fact that the rules are continually changing make it impossible for anyone to have an accurate grasp of what it is all about?

A. Knowledge can be acquired through training courses, written information etc., and there are a range of experts and specialist welfare rights groups who can offer advice.

Q. Aren't people with learning disabilities and their carers afraid of losing benefits?

A. Yes, but these worries can be addressed if you talk with them about this and develop your own knowledge and expertise about benefits.

Three steps for tackling benefit issues

1 Familiarise yourself with the current benefits (and any other income) which the person is receiving and anything else which might affect their benefit entitlement (e.g. where the person lives; other sources of income in the household; and any previous difficulties in claiming benefits). Even this may not be straightforward. The person may be receiving one or more of ten different benefits, in varying combinations, one of several levels of payment of a benefit, and from more than one office. There is no procedure for obtaining a simple written breakdown of a person's full entitlement to benefits. On the plus side, more information is now included in benefits books and in leaflets from the Benefits Agency. Most importantly, the majority of individuals will be receiving the same combination of benefits – severe disablement allowance, income support and disability living allowance – so concentrate on these and seek expert advice about the rest.

2 Consider how the proposed change in circumstances will affect the person's existing benefit entitlement and whether they could claim alternative/additional benefits such as Disability Working Allowance, which would increase their overall income. Each benefit has its own set of rules about earnings and although the effect on benefits for users of a proposed employment service cannot be guaranteed absolutely, it is possible to be reasonably certain and revise the service accordingly if necessary. On this basis, individuals can make an informed choice about whether to change their daytime activities.

3 Check the wider financial implications of changing the person's income and benefit status. A number of other issues can influence a decision on whether to change their benefit entitlement. Some are positive (e.g. easier access to credit as an earner). In other instances any gain from earned income could be more than offset by something like health problems necessitating high prescription costs, or reduced income because of regular periods of sick leave. There could also be higher housing costs if the person is living independently or if their carers receive help with rent or council tax charges.

One obvious matter to consider is how benefit entitlement will be affected if the person's employment ceases. In some cases, a supported-employment service can plan for this: e.g. entitlement to disability working allowance can protect a person's right to reclaim severe disablement allowance or incapacity benefit for up to two years.

WORKED EXAMPLE

A person over the age of 25, living at home with family carer (who receives invalid care allowance of £38.70 but no other benefits). The person receives total benefits of £119.70 (1998/9 rates):

	£
Severe Disablement Allowance	52.70
Income Support	19.10
Disability Living Allowance (Care) (middle rate)	34.30
Disability Living Allowance (Mobility) (low rate)	13.60

These benefits have differing rules about work and earnings:

- The incapacity benefit (SDA) is covered by 'therapeutic earnings' which allow the person weekly earnings of up to £48.00 plus expenses (and maximum 16 hours in some contexts).
- The means-tested benefit (income support) is covered by an income disregard of £15.00 (no expenses).
- There is no specific provision about work for DLA; the award is based on the claimant's care/mobility needs.

The effect of increasing hours of work and earnings, in simple terms:

Earnings	Impact of Earnings	Income = Earnings plus
Up to £15.00	Accepted as therapeutic; no effect on earnings	SDA, IS & DLA
£15.00–£34.10	IS would be reduced by the amount of earnings above £15; so no increase in weekly income	SDA, reduced IS, and DLA
£34.10–£48.00	If work accepted as therapeutic, then income derived from SDA and earnings, but loss of IS affects entitlements like free prescriptions	SDA & DLA
£48.00 plus	No entitlement to SDA. If working 16 or more hours, could claim DWA; on returning order book to Benefits Agency would have to submit separate request to DLA Unit to continue payment of DLA (and ICA)	DWA & DLA
Up to £147.00	Could be entitled to award of DWA, max. £61.55 reducing as earnings increase; would also ensure free prescriptions etc. and possible right to reclaim SDA within two years	DWA & DLA

SDA – Severe Disablement Allowance
IS – Income Support
DLA – Disability Living Allowance
DWA – Disability Working Allowance

Maxim supported employment brokerage

Maxim is a newly established brokerage service, funded by Liverpool City Council, Liverpool Health Authority and Merseyside Training and Enterprise Council and is managed by a board of representatives from each agency. Two brokers are employed, both of whom have substantial experience in supported employment.

Aims

Maxim aims to assist supported-employment providers to:

◆ access secure and strategic funding;

◆ improve their staff recruitment, training and retention;

◆ develop effective and efficient supported-employment models;

◆ find and maintain good paid jobs for people with learning disabilities;

◆ monitor and evaluate their provision.

They will also work directly with people with learning disabilities who are seeking work by advising them on available support services.

Tasks

Maxim has set itself a range of tasks, including the following.

◆ Encouraging and supporting the promotion of supported employment with other day services and working with them to promote employment opportunities.

◆ Developing and co-ordinating the efficient and effective purchasing of appropriate vocational or supported-employment services for people with learning disabilities.

◆ Raising the profile of supported employment with employers.

◆ Monitoring employers' requirements and developing effective recruitment services which are responsive to these requirements.

◆ Establishing a common definition and quality standard between purchasers and providers and developing an acceptable system of accreditation.

◆ Encouraging agencies providing supported employment to work together.

◆ Establishing a database recording the employment of people with learning disabilities and identifying gaps in the provision of supported employment or the need for further development.

Contact: Maxim, Merseyside TEC, Tithebarn House, Tithebarn Street, Liverpool L2 2NZ. Tel: 0151 236 0026; fax: 0151 236 4013.

Useful contacts

Association of Supported Employment Agencies (ASEA), Pat McNeil, Area Secretariat, Cheshire CC, Supported Employment, Central Offices, Hartford Business Centre, Chester Road, Hartford, Northwich, Cheshire CW8 2AB. Tel: 01606 301027.

ASEA was formed in 1991. It acts as a focus for continuing improvement in supported-employment practice and the development of national policies by government and organisations involved in promoting the paid employment of people with learning disabilities. There are active regional groups.

Training in Systematic Instruction (TSI), Ashleigh, Sunnyside, Todmorden, Lancs PL14 7AP. Tel: 01706 813555. e-mail: tsi@mcr1.poptel.org.uk

Further reading

Callahan, M. (1992), 'Job Site Training and Natural Supports' in J.Nisbet (ed.), *Natural Supports in School, at Work and in the Community for People with Severe Disabilities.* Baltimore, MD: Paul H. Brookes, pp. 257–76.

Lister, T., Ellis, L., Phillips, T., O'Bryan, A., Beyer, S. and Kilsby, M. (1992), *Survey of Supported Employment Services in England, Scotland and Wales.* Manchester: National Development Team.

McLoughlin, C.S., Garner, J.B and Callahan, M.J. (eds) (1987), *Getting Employed, Staying Employed.* Baltimore, MD: Paul H. Brookes.

O'Bryan, A and O'Brien, J. (1995), *Supported Employment Quality Assurance.* Manchester: National Development Team.

Pozner, A. and Hammond, J. (1994), *An Evaluation of Supported Employment Initiatives for Disabled People.* Employment Department Research Series No. 17. Sheffield: Employment Department.

Wertheimer, A. (1991), *Making It Happen. Employment opportunities for people with severe learning difficulties.* London: King's Fund.

Wertheimer, A. (1993), *Changing Lives: Supported employment and people with learning disabilities.* Manchester: National Development Team.

Chapter 6

Creating inclusive communities

Vision and principles

The vision of inclusive communities where everyone belongs is very different from the experiences of community of most people with learning disabilities who have traditionally been marginalised or excluded completely. A vision of inclusiveness will demand major shifts in the way we think and act – as individuals, in organisations and as members of our local communities.

The challenge for all of us is to create communities based on co-operation and interdependence, where everyone is seen as having a contribution to make and where people's differences are acknowledged and valued rather than being a reason for rejecting them.

Moving towards creating inclusive communities will involve:

- *challenging our current ways of thinking and exploring more radical new ideas;*
- *living and working in systems which offer much less security and certainty and being prepared to take risks;*
- *understanding that inclusion is an ongoing process;*
- *moving away from hierarchical structures and towards partnership;*
- *sharing responsibility for defining vision and purpose between all the stakeholders;*
- *developing new skills in listening and advocacy;*
- *confronting and discussing prejudice and oppression;*
- *shifting from control to empowerment.*

The current scene

We are beginning to see small but nonetheless significant changes for some individuals but still too often we continue to segregate large sectors of the community from the mainstream of life, congregating people because they are elderly or impaired or otherwise labelled as different. In doing so, we impoverish everyone by excluding people who have a positive contribution to make.

The reality for the majority of people with learning disabilities is that they spend most of their time with their own families, other people with disabilities or people paid to be with them. They lack the wider social networks of friends, acquaintances and workmates which most of us take for granted.

What this means for managers

Managers need to create an organisational culture committed to full inclusion of people with learning disabilities regardless of their degree of disability. This should be part of the service's vision for the future, understood and taken on board by everyone in the service. But vision alone is not enough. The organisation needs to turn the vision into reality: we have 'talked the talk', now it is time to 'walk the walk'. Inclusion needs to be embedded in every part of the organisation. It cannot be left to the 'access officer' or the 'volunteer co-ordinator': it is everybody's business and everyone's responsibility.

Checklist for managers

Staff recruitment

◆ Recruit individuals who demonstrate a commitment to inclusion and an understanding of what that involves.

◆ Look for staff whose frame of reference is community-based rather than service-oriented.

◆ Look for personal qualities such as maturity, creativity, sound judgement, common sense, sensitivity, a natural instinct for hospitality and a willingness to persevere. These are particularly important qualities to look for when recruiting front-line staff.

◆ Look out for people who are well established in the local community where they will be working, who know where the real influence is, who the opinion formers are and who they can call on to get things done.

Training and development

◆ Organise training which encourages staff to see services as a stepping-stone to helping individuals strengthen and increase their social networks with people in the community.

◆ Recognise that some staff will feel they have lost their role as 'service providers' and help them understand the exciting new contribution they can make in enabling people to lead lives which are based in real community rather than in special services.

◆ Encourage staff to develop supportive relationships with one another rather than seeing themselves as part of a hierarchical structure where they always rely on more senior staff for advice and support.

Uncertainty and risk

◆ Managers need to support staff in taking more risks, allowing for more risk-taking while still ensuring the safety of vulnerable people.

◆ Job descriptions can be written to give staff greater freedom to increase people's opportunities to spend more time outside segregated 'safe' settings.

Timescales for developing networks

◆ Recognise that long-term and sustained effort is required to begin to foster the kind of relationships in people's lives which have a good chance of being permanent or at the very least long-term.

◆ Take time to help a person acquire a network which has sufficient people in it to survive and renew itself even when some of that network will come and go.

◆ One-to-one relationships are valuable and some projects have fostered these, but if the relationship breaks down it can leave the person again with no one significant in their life. The 'link' person should be seen as just that – someone who helps the person with learning disabilities link up with other people and widen their social networks.

> **Sustained funding**
>
> ◆ Avoid short-term or 'special project' funding. This puts pressure on workers to get 'good numbers' (rather than good relationships for people).
>
> ◆ Lack of ongoing funding can lead to tokenistic, superficial work which rarely results in lasting and substantial change in people's lives.
>
> ◆ A service which is costly initially in terms of staff time and seems slow to get off the ground may be more economical in the long run as people become genuinely less dependent on services and real community involvement begins to take hold.

What this means for front-line staff

There are many ways in which front-line staff can help people develop networks of relationships and participate more widely in community life. Here are a few suggestions (and the reading list at the end of this chapter has others).

- Make a 'social assessment' of the person's interests, talents, skills and needs. How do they feel, function, respond and relate in a social sense and in non-institutional settings (e.g. pubs, shops, parties, other people's homes)?
- In your mind, go for possibilities first. Then think about risks and how to manage them. Take reasonable risks or you will never move anything on! If you find that difficult, ask yourself why. Are you too protective – too much in your 'service provider' role and not enough in companion mode? Does it feel like too much bother to you? Do you genuinely want to safeguard the person or are you protecting your own back?
- Be a detective: follow leads relating to the person's interests, see where they go and act on suggestions from local people. Ask people you meet if they know anything that could help and let them know that you want their views, opinions, comments and ideas. Have lunch with pensioners, go to an angling club, ask the local newsagent for information, chat with the café owner or pub manager, go backstage at your local theatre or drama society.
- Involve the person in as many aspects of planning and reviewing as possible such as making and receiving phone calls, deciding how to get to places, finding information, etc. You may need to break down an apparently simple task into several elements and

ask the person to do the bits they can. Try to support them to do things rather than automatically doing it yourself.

- Do not hover round the person: show the world that they are their own person. Let them take the initiative and speak for themselves as much as possible. Try to naturally get into conversation with people like shopkeepers, taxi drivers and café/theatre customers if you see they are interested in the person.

- Visit neighbourhood centres – preferably with the person. Meet staff and volunteers there and ask lots of questions. Ask what the person could contribute to local activities, e.g. helping on a stall at the local festival or fair, taking photographs of events. Find out whether the centre would be interested in setting up an integrated class, or a workshop or an exhibition.

- Look for suitable volunteering opportunities for the person (so long as it is not exploitative). It is a good way of meeting new people, as well as feeling useful and learning new skills. Your local volunteer bureau is often a good starting point.

- If an activity has a fee attached (e.g. swimming, using a gym) offer to pay the fee for a potential fellow participant. This enables people on low incomes to share their time on a regular basis when they might otherwise be unable to pursue a particular activity.

- If places the person goes to are not too far away, get to know a local minicab firm. Agree procedures for safety. Get to know some regular drivers. This can help ensure that as many people as possible can travel without escorts, pay their own fares, share cabs and (within reason) get help from drivers.

- Make sure you have enough time to reflect on what did or did not seem to work and why. Learn from experience so that you can tackle any practical, psychological and other barriers to integration.

What this means for carers

Parents and other family members are usually the foundation on which a person's links to the local community are built. Most parents will welcome a service which offers their son or daughter new challenges and opportunities in the community and means less time in segregated settings. They are generally prepared to live with a degree of anxiety about risk and uncertainty because they recognise the potential benefits of their son or daughter exploring the world beyond the 'safety' of the day centre.

Parents may be prepared to take an active role themselves in developing these new opportunities. In Havering (Essex), for example, they took a lead in organising the transport for the new daytime service and in Belfast parents set up their own project to develop job opportunities because they were dissatisfied with the limited existing services at their local day centre.

However, some parents may be less convinced that inclusion is the right way to proceed. Years of pessimistic predictions from professionals, sometimes combined with negative reactions from people in the community, may have left them feeling pessimistic or lacking the energy to seek change for their son or daughter. They may find it hard to believe that things could be different. For others, caring may have become so central to their lives that the dependency is mutual; they may block all attempts to help their relative get out and about more. Parents in this situation will need sensitive and patient support from professionals but may also find it helpful to talk with other parents who have had similar fears and anxieties.

Carers my find it helpful to rethink their son's or daughter's connections with other relatives or with neighbours and friends.

Sheena is a young woman with multiple disabilities. A link worker spent a lot of time getting to know her and her family. Gradually her family began to see her in a new light. They took more interest and included her in more of their own lives and in the wider community.

Through her circle of friends, Mary discovered a large long-lost family, including a sister who had never been asked to be involved in Mary's life and didn't think she had anything to offer until she was asked!

A new look at the people in someone's life may uncover unrecognised possibilities for community connections.

With the help of a couple of friends, Matthew drew a map of the people in his life. One of these was a worker at the local church who he saw every Friday evening. When his mother saw the map she said: 'Oh, I never thought of him!'

It sometimes takes courage to ask other family members or friends to become involved in a person's life but parents and other family members who have taken that risk have ended up with new and previously unimagined people in their son's or daughter's network.

What this means for users

Many more people with learning disabilities are now getting out and about in the community, taking part in a wide range of activities at colleges and leisure centres and doing voluntary work. Some people are now out doing something different almost every evening. But much of this is still segregated group activity: few have moved on to activities open to anyone in the community.

A sizeable number do not even have these opportunities; often they are people who need a lot of support to 'give it a go'. If you have attended a day centre for years you may be afraid of trying out new things and have never had the chance to develop your sense of curiosity which often leads on to new experiences. You may not feel confident or believe you can learn. All this can make it difficult to imagine a different lifestyle.

You may need help to make choices and want to try out various activities. Taster days and sessions are a good idea but sometimes it takes longer to make up your mind about whether you enjoy something. Having a go at something with a friend can be a good way of exploring new avenues.

Small pockets of good practice around the country are changing the lives of a few people. Our challenge is to make that good practice universal!

'I went to Leavesden Hospital in 1949 and stayed there. Time was short for starting a job when I came out because of my age. I went to a conference about supported work. I got a job just after that in Marks & Spencer and worked there for four years till I retired. I was very proud to work for M&S. I lived for my work nearly. Everyone was very worried about me retiring and what I would do to make up for M&S. I was really uptight about missing it.

To start with, Rosemary got my friend Paul and me to invite all my other friends together one evening and over coffee and biscuits we started my circle of friends. Since then I have not looked back. My circle of friends meets about every six weeks and we plan what we'll do together. Last summer we went out on trips to the canal and to pubs.

The first time we met was in a church hall as my friends didn't know each other. Now we meet in different houses. From my circle I have joined the Baptist Church house group to study the Bible and I joined the National Trust as I like visiting their places. I go to the Arts Society with Maureen. I am writing my life story with Brian. He visits each week. We make notes and he types them up. Maureen is doing pen and ink sketches for my story and I'm taking photos. I met Maureen when working in M&S. Barry is in my circle and Helga, his wife, has joined too. We all bring along something to eat and wine. We talk about what to do and where to go, and have a good laugh.

I have asked one or two more people to join my circle but mostly it is the eight of us. We all ring each other up and do things each week till we all get together again. Paul keeps us together with help from Sandra. I can talk in my circle better than anywhere else. They really listen to me and do not go up in the air.

My advice to anyone who wants to start a circle of friends is to go round and ask and keep asking – they'll come if they want to. Circles are good for retirement but they would be good if you were five or sixty-five. I would be lost without my circle.'

Circles Network

The aim of Circles Network is to build inclusive communities where everyone belongs. One way of achieving greater inclusion for people who are marginalised is to develop a network or circle of support. This is not a one-to-one befriending or advocacy scheme but the bringing together of a group of people who care about and are committed to the person who has invited them to form a circle.

Most people have a personal and natural network of others in their lives; with circles this network of people is brought together to work actively with the 'focus person'. Together the group organises and plans to make change happen, following the dreams of that person and supporting each other in the process.

The emphasis is on equality so circle members are not 'volunteers' or 'befrienders'. No one is paid to take part although the focus person may need a paid facilitator to take the lead and get the circle started.

Contact: Circles Network, Pamwell House, 160 Pennywell Road, Upper Easton, Bristol BS5 0TX. Tel: 0117 939 3917; fax: 0117 939 3918.

The Access Project, Camden

Access is primarily for people who lack valued relationships of their own making – people who only have contact with service providers or stay at home for most of the time and thus have limited opportunities for finding and building relationships in the community in which they live.

The project assists people with learning disabilities to be involved in their communities on equal terms. Members of the community are seen as the project's natural partners and its greatest resource.

The project helps establish networks of support and friendships in people's social, cultural and working lives. It is not a befriending scheme but a bridge for people into ordinary life. It introduces people with learning disabilities to new experiences and opportunities for choice and involvement which can enable them to continue with activities and relationships once Access is no longer involved in their lives.

Access has a paid co-ordinator who supports sessional workers and community members but it is this latter group who play the key role. Anyone can become involved: all they need is openness, a willingness to learn with others and to give a relationship with someone with a learning disability the same chance as any other relationship they might make. Access seeks to reflect the cultural and ethnic backgrounds of people in the local community and aims to have a roughly equal number of men and women users.

Contact: Access Project, 45 Cromwell Avenue, London N6 5HP. Tel: 0171 485 8177 (messages only for Sharon Lytton).

In Otley, Leeds, people with learning disabilities are getting involved in a community play, an event involving the whole community and stretching over a period of 18 months. Creating, producing and staging a play provides many opportunities for integrated activities, including a choir, and music and drama workshops.

Contact: Sharing Care, Oxford Chambers, Oxford Place, Leeds LS1 3AX. Tel: 01132 470411.

Avenues to Opportunity is a community placement service for adults with physical and learning disabilities, funded by Sunderland Social Services. Avenues offer adults with disabilities the opportunity to explore and participate in the life of their local communities through various recreational, social, educational or voluntary pursuits. Avenues achieves this by providing short-term support, based on individual need, through one-to-one links with other members of the community. Support is provided by paid sessional support workers.

Avenues currently employs eighteen support workers supporting 21 service users. A recruitment drive is in process to appoint 10–15 additional support workers and an assistant manager to the service. Since Avenues became operational in July 1995, 63 people have been successful in using the service where support has been withdrawn and they have continued to attend their activity.

Contact: Avenues to Opportunity, 12–13 Toward Road, Sunderland, SE1 2QF. Tel: 0191 553 7356. Fax: 0191 553 7360.

Further reading

Billingham, N. and Daniel, J. (1992), 'Leisure – a serious business', *Llais*, Spring 1992, Cardiff: SCOVO.

Block, P. (1994), *Stewardship: Choosing service over self-interest.* San Francisco, CA: Berett Koehler Publishers.

De Pree, M. (1989), *Leadership Is an Art*. London: Arrow Books.

Hayes, L. (1994/5), 'Trying together', *Community Care,* 22 Dec 1994–5 Jan 1995, pp. 20–21.

King's Fund Centre (1988), *Ties and connections. An ordinary community life for people with learning difficulties.* London: King's Fund.

Ludlum, C (1993), *Tending the Candle. A booklet for circle facilitators.* Manchester, Connecticut: Communitas.

McKnight, J.L. and Kretzmann, J.P. (1993), *Building Communities from the Inside Out. A path towards finding and mobilising a community's assets*. Illinois: Centre for Urban Affairs of Policy Research.

Minnesota Developmental Disabilities Council (1994), *Shifting Patterns*. Minnesota: DD Council.

Parents with Attitude (1996), *Let Our Children Be. A collection of stories.* Compiled by P. Murray and J. Penman. Sheffield: Parents with Attitude.

Rajan, V. (1993), *Rebuilding Communities. Experiences and experiments in Europe.* Totnes, Devon: Green Books.

Richardson, A, and Ritchie, J. (1989), *Developing Friendships: Enabling people with learning disabilities to make and maintain friends.* PSI Research Report No. 697, London: Policy Studies Institute. (Includes comprehensive bibliography)

Snow, J. (1992), *The Inclusion Papers.* Toronto: Inclusion Press.

Wertheimer, A. (1995), *Circles of Support. Building inclusive communities.* Bristol: Circles Network.

Chapter 7

Planning for individuals

Vision and principles

We are still too caught up in thinking that the needs of people with disabilities can only be met by services and by what professionals can offer with the result that many people still rely on paid services in every aspect of their lives: where they live, who they live with, who they spend their time with and what they do.

It could be argued that individual planning is unnecessary. After all, most people do not have a written plan for their lives. It is not very 'ordinary'. But there are sound reasons why we need individual person-centred plans:

- *people have often followed the same programme for years without any significant changes. Few of us make no changes at all in our lives;*
- *without some form of individual planning, people with little or no speech may have no means of making their wishes known;*
- *without plans there may be no impetus to help people makes changes in their lives. Writing plans helps everyone make a commitment to change;*
- *an individual plan is a way of looking at the whole person, rather than viewing them as a series of 'needs' – for residential, day or leisure services.*

Background

Individual planning for people with learning disabilities is not a new idea. In the past people had 'treatment plans' or 'case plans' and by the late 1970s we had 'Individual Programme Plans' or 'Individual Service Plans' (IPPs and ISPs). Today there are a variety of ways of looking at individual people, including 'whole life planning', 'lifestyle planning', 'personal futures planning' and 'essential life planning'.

Although names change and different approaches are developed, it is important to identify what is central to truly person-centred planning and how this differs from traditional planning and the statutory processes of assessment and case management.

What person-centred planning is not about

For a number of reasons, attempts to develop person-centred planning have not always made a positive difference to people's lives:

- planning becomes an assessment of what people cannot do, services are enlisted to remedy 'deficits' and people are never considered quite 'ready' for ordinary life;
- key people in the individual's life such as relatives, friends and front-line staff who know them best are not always involved in planning – though they are often expected to implement other people's plans;
- plans are based on existing provision, sometimes because planning takes place within the context of a service, making it harder for people to free their minds to explore more creative and less service-based options;
- planning is carried out by professionals rather than in partnership with the person concerned;
- too little time is spent really getting to know the person well enough to make the process meaningful. There is no sense of the person as a human being and of what they want out of life.

The essentials of person-centred planning

Effective planning will depend to some extent on a person's individual circumstances but we know from experience that there are some common elements that need to be taken on board if the process is to result in positive changes in people's lives.

- *Ensure the individual is central.* It is essential to find ways of actively engaging the person directly in the planning process. This requires imagination and a willingness to experiment with different ways of communicating other than in the usual 'meeting' format. It means moving away from a pattern of meetings in offices or other formal settings and being in more familiar settings where the person feels comfortable such as their own home.

- *Involve people's networks.* Even people whose lives seem very 'service-based' are likely to have important networks of relatives, friends, neighbours, support workers, etc. Sometimes these networks come together as a circle of support (see Chapter 6). Planning might be in a circle of this kind or through a more formal support system although the latter needs to be in close touch with the individual's network if effective life plans are to be developed and implemented.

- *Focus on strengths and capacities.* Everyone has some strengths and the capacity to develop new ones. Focusing on what people can and would like to do offers positive direction and hope. This does not mean ignoring difficulties in people's lives but looking at how existing and potential strengths can challenge them.

- *Create a vision for the future.* We need to gain a sense of what an individual would like to be and do. These hopes and dreams have often been dismissed as 'unrealistic' even though most of us have dreams for the future. Dreams or visions are integral to the process of helping someone shape their own future rather than having it determined by paid services.

- *Develop a personal profile.* An important starting-point for thinking about the future is having a sense of who someone is now and what their current life is like. In order to involve the person actively in this process it may be helpful to think of using things like posters, photos, videos and life-story books rather than just the written word.

- *Start with achievable short-term goals.* It can help enormously if some goals – large or small – are achieved early on. This can encourage everyone to tackle the more challenging aspects of an individual plan, the goals which seem more difficult to attain.

- *Keep things under review.* Person-centred planning is not a one-off exercise or something only carried out every year or two or when a crisis occurs. Keep an eye on how things are changing all the time, bring in new people if that seems appropriate. Effective person-centred planning will make space for reflection and renewal.

Person-centred planning and day services

For many individuals, staff in day services are the people they see most of other than their carers: service users often spend many hours with day centre staff on a regular basis. The day service is also frequently the only context in which any individual planning occurs – through review meetings, for example. However, because day services do not always have access to other resources, plans may be based wholly or largely around what the day centre can offer.

Despite these difficulties, in many ways day services staff are in a strong position to carry out effective individual planning because of their knowledge and understanding of individuals, sometimes over quite long periods of time. In order for planning to be effective, though, it must involve the person's family and social networks.

Individual planning within day services needs to be undertaken in close collaboration with staff operating statutory assessment and case management systems. The active support of senior managers is also crucial. If centres are working out what individuals want and supporting them in a range of activities outside the centre rather than providing everything within their own buildings then changes to the pattern of services need to be acknowledged.

A way forward

'None of us makes our life alone. We each rely on a variety of formal and informal resources to create better life experiences . . . People with severe disabilities count on more able people's planning and organising skills for help to identify and co-ordinate resources to meet life's challenges.' John O'Brien (1987)

Some kind of individual person-centred planning process makes this possible. It places at the heart of all planning people's relationships and the value of self-esteem and personal empowerment through informed and supported choice and opportunities. Day services could provide the planning and organising skills John O'Brien describes to make this a reality.

The MAPS Mandala

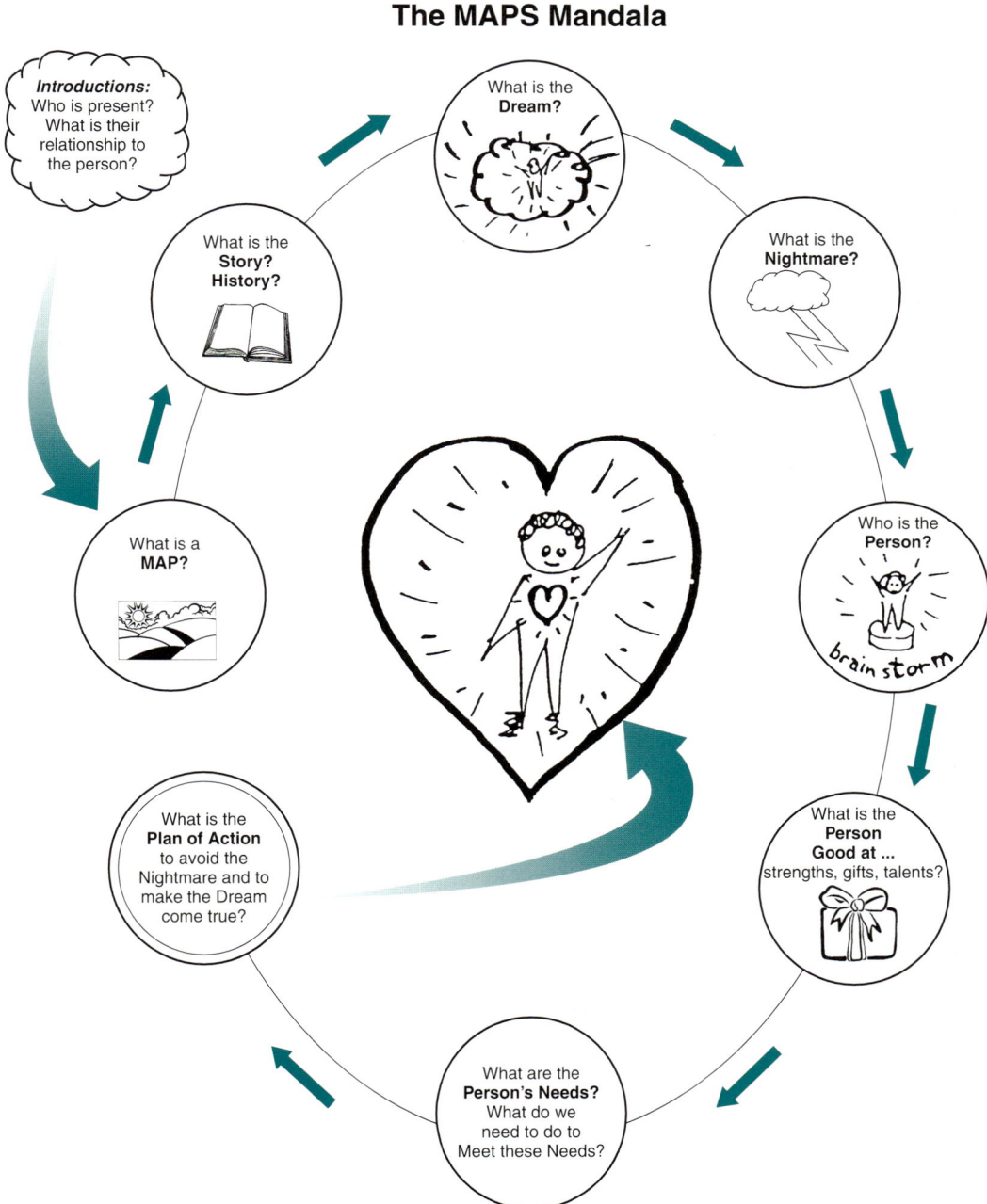

Introductions: Who is present? What is their relationship to the person?

What is the **Story? History?**

What is the **Dream?**

What is the **Nightmare?**

What is a **MAP?**

Who is the **Person?** brainstorm

What is the **Plan of Action** to avoid the Nightmare and to make the Dream come true?

What is the **Person Good at ...** strengths, gifts, talents?

What are the **Person's Needs?** What do we need to do to Meet these Needs?

Further reading

Allen, W. (1987), *Read My Lips: It's my choice*. Minnesota Governor's Planning Council on Developmental Disabilities, Minnesota.

Minnesota Governor's Planning Council on Developmental Disabilities (1992), *Shifting Patterns*. Minnesota Governor's Planning Council on Developmental Disabilities, Minnesota.

Mount, B., Ducharme, G. and Beeman, P. (1991), *Person-Centred Development: A journey in learning to listen to people with disabilities*. Manchester, CT: Communitas.

Mount, B. and Zwewrnik, K. (1989), *It's Never Too Early, Never Too Late. A book about personal futures planning*. Publisher and place of publication?

O'Brien, J. (1987), 'A Guide to Personal Futures Planning'. In Bellamy T G, Wilcox B (eds). *A Comprehensive Guide to the Activities Catalogue. An alternative curriculum for youths and adults with severe disabilities*. Baltimore MD: Paul H Brookes.

Perske, R. and Perske, M. (1988), *Circles of Friends*. Nashville, TN: Abingdon Press.

Smull, M. and Harrison, S.B. (1992), *Supporting People with Severe Reputations in the Community*. Alexandria, VA: National Association of State Directors of Developmental Disabilities Inc., 113 Orinoco Street, Alexandria, VA 22314.

Chapter 8

Making it happen for people with the most complex disabilities

Vision and principles

Inclusion in the life of ordinary communities must be the goal for everyone with a disability, including those who may need intensive support in order to do so because of the complexity of their disabilities or because they behave in ways which may be risky and threatening to themselves and/or other people.

Service providers generally struggle to understand and meet their needs. However, we are learning more and more about how we can do this better. This chapter offers guidance and advice on how people who are difficult to serve can be included in new patterns of day services.

The current scene

People with challenging or problematic behaviour

This may include people who are aggressive or who injure themselves or otherwise behave in ways seen as anti-social. This is often an expression of feelings which cannot be (or are not) communicated verbally such as frustration, anger, boredom, resentment and a sense of rejection. Unfortunately, most service responses to date have led to more restrictions, more deprivation and less choice, setting up a vicious circle of escalating challenging behaviour. Trying to understand what feelings are being communicated through this behaviour and helping the person find other ways of making those feelings known can lead to positive changes and a reduction in challenging behaviour.

Pauline was moved to the Special Needs Unit of her day centre because she was becoming increasingly aggressive towards other people. Unfortunately Pauline didn't like the Unit's activities so became even more aggressive. Luckily staff guessed she was bored and started supporting her in an office job two days a week. Pauline really enjoys this job and after six months has shown no aggression at work although she can still be aggressive on the days she attends the Unit.

Challenging behaviour can sometimes be the way that the person has learned to get something they want and staff then need to teach them other ways of achieving their goals.

Peter used to hit himself on the head as a way of saying 'Leave me alone' or 'Give me a break'. With teaching, he has learned to use pictures to tell other people what he wants.

One way of learning how to deal with difficult situations is to watch how others cope in similar situations. When someone is in a segregated setting with people who have similar difficulties such role models are often not around which is one reason why it is so important for people to have opportunities for participating in ordinary activities in ordinary places.

Adrian used to treat women disrespectfully but since starting work he has been able to watch how his fellow workers interact with members of the opposite sex. As a result, his attitudes and behaviour towards women have become much more positive.

Contrary to what usually happens, people with challenging behaviour need more rather than fewer choices, and more opportunities to control their lives in terms of what they do, where they spend time and who they are with. Michael Smull's person-centred Essential Lifestyle Planning is a very useful way of understanding how a person would like to live their life and the supports they need to do this successfully.

It is important to acknowledge that providing more opportunities for being in ordinary settings can be risky and we are not suggesting throwing caution to the wind. People's health and safety must not be compromised, but they do need to be given the space and encouragement to take sensible risks and 'have a go'. This has implications for staff at all levels.

Staff were reluctant to take Mary out to restaurants as she tended to steal other people's food at the day centre. Once they had worked out what they would do if that happened in a restaurant they felt confident enough to try it for real and Mary surprised everyone by her impeccable table manners. One of the best ways of supporting people is to have high expectations of them.

Helping a person construct the lifestyle of their choice when they have very little personal experience to draw on takes patience and tenacity. We are not likely to get it right first time – and even if we do, people change.

When David started his new job he really enjoyed it and his job trainer thought David was 'settled'. Fourteen months later, David showed signs of boredom at work, making it clear that he wanted something different. His job trainer helped David find a new job and he is now settled in there. It was important to see the first job not as a 'failure' but as part of an ongoing process of meeting his needs.

Staff need to get to know the person really well, spending time with them in a variety of settings and sharing different activities. What are the person's likes and dislikes? What situations seem to trigger challenging behaviour? What do they find stressful or frustrating and how can this be avoided? What kind of people or situations seem to make them feel comfortable? For individuals from Black and minority ethnic groups, there may be cultural issues which need to be taken into account when thinking about the best way of supporting them. Taking time to really try and understand someone can allow them to build up confidence in relationships and enable staff to start developing strategies for coping with challenging behaviours.

There are no short-cuts or quick and easy ways of really understanding a person and finding out what makes them 'tick'. Services need to ensure that front-line staff are given as much time as they need for this. Managers have to resist pressure to produce quick results. The brief stories about individual people included in this chapter may make it all sound deceptively simple; the reality is that we try, do not always get it right, need to spend time reflecting on our experiences and try again (and again and again). We are not talking about 'fixing' a 'problem' but about an ongoing process and a continuing commitment to individuals.

Supporting someone in their chosen activities is largely about teaching new skills but not just in the rather narrow 'task teaching' sense (e.g. teaching someone how to shop). It involves teaching social skills such as when particular interactions are appropriate or how to make conversation, helping a person develop problem-solving abilities and helping them maintain appropriate control over their feelings. This kind of 'coaching' will help people begin to learn from their experiences so that inappropriate patterns of behaviour begin to change.

The last but probably most crucial factor in supporting people successfully is building good relationships between the support worker and the individual. Trying out new activities in new settings can be frightening for all concerned, but anxiety levels will be reduced if the person with challenging behaviours trusts the person supporting them. A relationship based on trust and mutual respect is often the key to helping someone give up their challenging behaviours and they are more likely to respond positively if they trust the person asking them to do so. Support staff, in turn, need to negotiate boundaries and be clear about what is or is not acceptable behaviour in a particular setting.

Experience has shown that when people can choose their own lifestyle with supports which are seen as enabling rather than controlling, problematic behaviour often diminishes. However, these difficulties have often been around for many years and so are unlikely to disappear overnight; it is a lengthy process of 'understanding, planning, doing, evaluating, trying to understand again ... Enlisting the help of a clinical psychologist, for example, can sometimes be useful where a person is finding it particularly difficult to change their behaviours. Accessing this kind of specialist help may not be easy but can make a real difference.

People with multiple disabilities

People with severe and complex disabilities usually spend their days in special care units where they receive considerable amounts of physical care but generally have few opportunities for community integration. A number of reasons are commonly cited for this, including: difficulties around management of epilepsy; the need for regular personal care; and limited physical access in community settings.

People with multiple disabilities have often been the last to leave long-stay hospitals which were closing down and are usually the least likely to be given access to new service initiatives. Unless we make a conscious effort they will be excluded or left at the end of the queue when more individualised daytime opportunities are being developed.

Like people with challenging behaviours, those with multiple disabilities can find it hard to make choices about their lives because of communication difficulties. Staff need to spend time with people in a variety of settings to 'tune in' to the way the person communicates non-verbally – often through subtle changes in vocal tone, posture or expression. They also need to take the time to understand a person's favoured routine which may be around something like eating or personal care and to support these positively. Again, Michael Smull's Essential Lifestyle Planning can help others understand the individual really well and so 'best guess' the sort of choices they would be likely to make.

Calculating and managing potential risk is important. Services generally focus on making people 'safe' and then figuring out what makes them happy in that setting, rather than starting with questions about 'happiness' and 'choice' and then working out what supports are needed to minimise risk.

Michael's seizures were so severe he was deemed 'not ready' for work, but his support worker realised that it could be a long time before they were more under control. The upshot was that the worker was trained to manage Michael's fits and cope with emergencies. Two years later Michael's seizures are still causing problems but they no longer prevent him going out and being in ordinary places with ordinary people.

Seeking advice from specialists such as speech or occupational therapists can help overcome some of the technical problems.

Margaret enjoyed her work in a large department store but her job trainer realised that her physical difficulties were preventing her carrying out some elements of the job. An occupational therapist was contacted who offered advice on positioning and on changing some of the routines. A speech therapist was also called in and helped Margaret develop a systematic way of communicating with co-workers using a picture dictionary and symbols. This made the whole experience much more satisfying for Margaret and her co-workers.

One of the biggest barriers for people with multiple disabilities is other people's belief that teaching and training should lead to full independence. This may be unrealistic for some people but should not stop us teaching people to perform parts of tasks or routines and offering help with those parts they cannot do. Sharing a task can be a mutually rewarding experience whether it is laying the table at home or operating a photocopier at work.

What this means for managers

People with the most complex needs must have the same access to an individualised service as others which means allowing staff to spend more time with individual clients. They will need skills, enthusiasm and patience so think about using staff who have these particular qualities.

It is important to promote a culture which allows staff to use their initiative and take calculated risks. Allow staff the space to learn from their mistakes and encourage creativity.

By working in partnership with health professionals who have specialist skills and knowledge, you can develop opportunities in ordinary settings with ordinary people.

Staff need access to relevant training such as systematic instruction, social role valorisation and augmentative communication.

What this means for front-line staff

A good service allows staff the time to work with people as people, to develop a clear understanding of how a person would like to live their life differently and will equip you with the skills and support to put some of those changes into practice.

What this means for users

People with complex disabilities are among the most vulnerable in society and we need to find ways of helping those who do not have a voice to communicate their needs and understand their rights. Independent advocacy (using citizen advocates, for example), is one important means of enabling someone's voice to be heard. Circles of support can also play an important advocacy role and have the added strength of enabling a group of people to share in supporting a vulnerable person. The self-advocacy movement too must continue to find ways of helping people who are at risk or being overlooked.

What this means for carers

Developing a vision of how someone might want to live their life is not always easy. Families have a vital part to play in helping service providers understand the person as they will probably know them better than anyone. They also need to be involved in drawing up plans and implementing new activities. They may need support to adjust to a more flexible service. Rather than a 9am to 3.30pm weekday service, their son or daughter may have a completely different 'schedule' which involves activities outside these hours but may also mean they are at home sometimes during the day. Where an individual's programme conflicts with their carers' own commitments, arrangements will have to be negotiated and mutually agreed.

> **Useful contacts**
>
> *Network, Liverpool. Contact: Jim Williams. Tel: 0151 250 3000, ext. 255.*
>
> This is a consortium of about ten supported-employment agencies in the city. A key focus is the joint mission statement endorsed by all members stating that no one should be excluded from employment because of their level of dependence, complexity of disability, or challenging behaviours. There are many examples of people with very complex and challenging disabilities who have been helped to obtain employment.
>
> *Chance to Work, Liverpool. Contact: Sue Branch. Tel: 0151 709 8368.*
>
> A supported-employment training agency provided by Barnardo's North West which offers a two-year training and supported-employment service for young adults with the most complex disabilities.
>
> *Sense UK, 11–13 Clifton Terrace, Finsbury Park, London N4 3SP. Tel: 0171 272 7774.*
>
> The National Deaf, Blind and Rubella Association for people who have dual sensory impairment and challenging behaviours. Sense have been working on ways of developing people's language and cognitive skills to enable them to spend more time in community settings.

References

Mansell, J. (1993), *Services for People with Learning Disabilities and Challenging Behaviour or Mental Health Needs: Report of a Project Group.* (Chairman: Professor J.L. Mansell). London: HMSO.

O'Brien, J. (1987), 'A Guide to Personal Futures Planning', in T.G. Bellamy, and B. Wilcox (eds), *A Comprehensive Guide to the Activities Catalogue. An alternative curriculum for youths and adults with severe disabilities.* Baltimore, MD: Paul H Brookes.

Puddicombe, B. (1995), *Face to Face: Communicating with people who do not use language.* London: Values into Action.

Smull, M. and Harrison, S.B. (1992), *Supporting People with Severe Reputations in the Community.* Alexandria, VA: National Association of State Directors of Developmental Disabilities Inc., 113 Orinoco Street, Alexandria, VA 22314.

Chapter 9

Black and minority ethnic issues

Vision and principles

Government community care policies recognise that 'people from different cultural backgrounds may have particular care needs ... [and] different concepts of community care.' They also acknowledge that 'good community care will take account of the circumstances of minority communities and will be planned in consultation with them'. As day services begin to offer more choice of activities in dispersed community settings, it is important that the needs of people with learning disabilities from Black and minority ethnic communities are properly considered. The planning and development of new forms of service provision must acknowledge and reflect the varied aspirations and concerns of multiracial, multicultural populations. Services which address the rights and needs of people with learning disabilities from Black and minority ethnic communities and those of their carers should be developed within the context of an overall race equality strategy which underpins the way the organisation operates. This strategy should include a set of standards which:

- *respects the privacy and dignity of the individual and his/her carers;*
- *acknowledges the individual needs of people with learning disabilities and their carers;*
- *caters for individuals' particular cultural and religious requirements;*
- *creates an environment which reflects people's cultural origins (e.g. pictures and 'ornamental dressings' or ornaments);*
- *provides opportunities for people to celebrate religious and/or cultural festivals and practise traditional customs;*
- *responds to and caters for difficulties in communication;*
- *provides access to professional bilingual and/or advocacy services;*
- *gives access to written information about services in the appropriate languages;*
- *makes clear how people can access complaints procedures.*

The current scene

People with learning disabilities from Black and minority ethnic communities often face 'double discrimination' through racism and the stigma of disability. This makes it doubly important that they are not further disadvantaged by new developments in day services. There is a need to avoid 'colour blind' planning which assumes that the concepts of community care appropriate to the majority population are equally relevant to other groups and their needs.

Current day centre provision often fails to cater for the needs of Black and minority ethnic service users. Inappropriate catering which ignores people's dietary requirements and food preferences is commonplace. Culturally appropriate activities, linking in with local Black and minority ethnic communities and their resources, are often lacking.

Black and minority ethnic workers are often under-represented in senior management positions. Although they should not automatically be seen as the 'experts' on all issues of race and culture, the outcome is often a 'colour blindness' – a lack of Black perspectives – at a strategic level which permeates services. It also fails to address the powerlessness of many Black staff and the very real discrimination which can occur in service systems.

Despite this, some providers are trying to address the issues and develop their day services in ways which are more responsive to users from minority ethnic communities and which reflect local cultural diversity. Others are aware that their provision is failing to meet the needs of Black and minority ethnic day service users but lack the support and advice to make changes.

Black and minority ethnic adults with learning disabilities are particularly disadvantaged in terms of finding employment. Like their non-disabled counterparts they face discrimination in the labour market and will require effective support and advocacy if they are to enter mainstream employment.

What this means for managers

The following checklist identifies key areas which managers need to address in developing day services which eliminate discrimination, promote equal access and which are developed within the context of a race equality strategy of the kind described above.

Checklist for managers

◆ Are there arrangements to identify the diversity of Black and minority ethnic populations, e.g. through analysis of the latest census information which can be used to inform development and provision of day services? Is this reviewed regularly?

◆ Does the service have arrangements for consulting with community organisations representing Black and minority ethnic groups about the range of daytime opportunities which needs to be developed and is their participation encouraged by using a range of methods appropriate to particular communities?

◆ What arrangements are in place for consulting with Black and minority ethnic service users, their families and representatives of community organisations on (a) planning new day services; (b) monitoring current provision; and (c) dissemination of information?

◆ Is there a budget which allows for the development of community contacts, can meet the information and training needs of Black and minority ethnic participants, and pays travel and childcare costs where necessary?

◆ Is there a training strategy for staff at all levels which promotes antiracist practice and considers the implications of developing services in a multiracial context?

◆ Does the service have a written policy on the provision of information in the languages of local minority ethnic communities? Is the policy clear about what information needs to be translated, how the translations will be commissioned and from whom, and how the quality of this information will be monitored and reviewed? Is this information available in a range of media such as leaflets, audiotapes and video-cassettes? Does information use clear, simple language and signs, pictures and symbols?

◆ Does the service have a policy detailing how day services will cater for the dietary requirements of people from Black and minority ethnic communities? Does the information make clear who is responsible for implementing the policy, for ensuring that the necessary information is provided to catering managers and suppliers, for organising staff training, and for translating menus?

◆ Are guidelines available to staff about respecting and catering for the differing religious and spiritual needs of service users and how they can help people access the religious and spiritual supports of their choice?

What this means for front-line staff

Staff development and training will play a key role in the delivery of services which are sensitive to the needs of users from Black and minority ethnic communities. Front-line staff must have access to training which addresses antiracist attitudes: simply providing 'information' about other cultures will not challenge antiracist practices.

Black and minority ethnic staff are commonly marginalised and unsupported. Their perspectives, knowledge and skills are often undervalued, even though they may be particularly well placed to develop new community-based activities for service users from similar backgrounds.

Black and minority ethnic staff will often have links to local community groups and organisations which could be tapped to enable individual service users to spend more time outside the day centre in culturally appropriate activities.

However, Black and minority ethnic staff should not be seen as 'race experts', which allows other staff to ignore their own responsibility in this area. Someone with the same cultural background may, for example, be able to welcome a new or potential service user but they should not necessarily assume ongoing responsibility for them.

What this means for carers

The majority of Black and minority ethnic people with learning disabilities live at home with their families who often cope with little support from services. Help that is offered is frequently based on false assumptions or misconceptions about the role of families as carers: e.g. that families 'prefer to look after their own' and automatically have extensive and supportive family networks.

Black and minority ethnic carers can find it difficult to access services for the person with a learning disability and for themselves. There may be language barriers. Awareness of racist attitudes in the community may also inhibit carers from seeking help, afraid of being seen as 'scroungers'.

Information and consultation strategies (see above) must address this issue. Listening to carers and gaining an understanding of individual families' needs and wishes will be crucial in developing appropriate supports.

What this means for users

People First has developed a charter of rights for Black service users which clearly sets out what Black people with learning disabilities want. This includes the rights to:

- be treated the same as everybody else;
- speak for myself and in my own language if I choose;
- learn about my culture and my history;
- wear the clothes I want to;
- choose my key worker and my social worker.
- have Black and white staff in day centres.

The Anika Patrice Project

The Anika Patrice Project was formed in 1991 because parents of young adults with learning disabilities in the London Borough of Hackney were concerned about the lack of support services for families from Black and minority ethnic communities. This was a particular problem in the evenings and at weekends and for families whose son or daughter had severe learning disabilities.

Initially families met together informally as a self-help group. One of the first issues they looked at was the myth that African, Caribbean and Asian families can cope with their disabled relatives within the family structure by using informal support. This myth, they decided, needed to be dispelled if people were to get the support services they badly needed.

The Project aims to:

◆ adopt a positive action approach to equal opportunities;

◆ respond to the differing cultural needs of the young people and their families and enhance the quality of their lives;

◆ provide training, educational opportunities and leisure activities for young people with learning disabilities, particularly from the African, Caribbean and Asian communities;

◆ offer support, advice, information and respite to carers.

In 1993, the project received joint funding which has enabled it to employ a small staff, including several sessional workers who have developed a programme of activities for the young people and particularly those with high support needs. There is a strong emphasis on culturally sensitive activities whether individually tailored or undertaken as a group.

Contact: Anika Patrice Project, 55 Albion Grove, London N16 8RE. Tel: 0171 923 9033.

References

Baxter, C., Poonia, K., Ward, L. and Nadirshaw, Z. (1990), *Double Discrimination: Issues and services for people with learning difficulties from Black and minority ethnic communities.* London: King's Fund.

Gunaratnam, Y. (1993), *Checklist Health and Race. A starting point for managers on improving services for Black populations.* London: King's Fund Centre.

People First (1994), *The Black People First Conference Report.* London: People First.

Chapter 10

Staff development

Vision and principles

'The health of the organisation and the quality of the service delivered will depend *considerably on the learning and development of its main resource: the staff.'* Sawden (1995)

Many of the best ideas about changing day services and some of the best innovative practice have come from managers and staff in day centres. This should not surprise us. Staff have much to contribute through skilled help in assisting people with learning disabilities; and their knowledge about the local community.

A day service which realises the potential of its staff will:

- *find ways of involving them in redesigning the service to better meet people's needs;*
- *support them in coming to terms with the change in role this will entail;*
- *enable them to learn the necessary skills the new service demands;*
- *support them in putting these new skills into practice.*
- *help them to draw on their individual skills, interests and aspirations.*

The current scene

The current situation is far from ideal. Many staff working in day services lack any formal qualification and have received little in-service training to help them take on board new ideas. Management styles are often traditional with front-line staff having little opportunity to participate in discussions about change and development to the service.

The role of day centres and thus of their staff has changed and broadened over the years. Staff can find they are expected to be teachers, sports trainers, group facilitators, activity developers, job finders, social skills trainers and many other things. They may have to take on roles for which they have had no relevant training or experience and previously relevant skills may no longer be needed. Day centre populations are changing too with more users having severe disabilities and complex needs.

At the same time, financial constraints mean that opportunities for in-service training are decreasing. Despite this, there are many instances where staff are overcoming these difficulties and playing a leading role in change. The challenge for the Changing Days project is to learn from these experiences and promote effective staff development which can lead to effective changes in the lives of people with learning disabilities.

What this means for managers

The following factors can be a useful 'agenda' for discussions with day service staff.

Motivation for change

People must actively want things to be different if change is to happen.

- Who is wanting to make changes and what is that about?
- Is change being introduced for 'external' reasons (e.g. a political decision to close down a centre)?
- Are there people other than staff who might also want things to be different?
- Can alliances be forged between those wanting change who are within the service and those outside with similar aspirations?
- Can key opinion-formers within the service draw others into the enterprise?
- Can factors which could inhibit or prevent change either within or outside the service be identified and their effects be reduced?

Values

A clear set of values, to which staff are committed, is an essential prerequisite for establishing clear outcomes for users.

- What is the values base of your service?
- Does it have coherent aims and definitions of desirable outcomes for people with learning disabilities and is it clear what staff need to do to achieve them?
- Are you sharing your own vision with staff?
- Are you available for staff to discuss your vision and share their own?

Building on

Staff need to feel that the service has already achieved things for people and that future developments will be adding to and enhancing these. If they feel that change implies everything that has happened to date is worthless, they may feel too devalued and deskilled to build on what has already been achieved. Training has to be an integral part of change.

- Are there any negative feelings around about change?
- Do they stem from fear of the unknown or complacency, or is there some other reason?
- Are staff aware of what the service has already achieved and how this can be built on?
- What do people want to change and develop and what would they like to remain the same?
- Is it possible to start up a local learning set in your locality with people from other services who are also wanting to make changes and is there someone who could act as facilitator?
- Do you do any team-building work and if so, how and in what ways?
- Do people see themselves as a necessary and integral part of a larger organisation and do they share the vision and values of that organisation and feel they can play a part in making that vision a reality?

A healthy and varied perspective

Staff can find it helpful to extend their horizons beyond the current day service and consider a range of alternatives. Avoid stereotyped thinking: we used to think everyone wanted to do music. Are we saying the same about employment now?

- Could staff and users do what they are doing in the current service elsewhere in the community?
- What opportunities do staff have to access new experiences and explore possible alternatives for users?
- Does your training budget enable staff to undertake individual study visits to innovative projects, etc.?
- Do staff know what the local community offers, particularly if they do not live in the area?
- Do staff have access to any shared training which could offer informal contact with other disciplines and the chance to learn about other services and their agendas?
- Would it be feasible to second staff to other projects for a time?
- Do staff have access to training which could help them integrate users into mainstream community activities?
- Are some staff so embedded in the 'service culture' that they see themselves primarily as 'professionals' rather than as ordinary human beings with their own life in the community?

Helping staff live with change

- What keeps staff going at stressful times, individually and as a team?
- What opportunities are there for people to have fun, be creative and renew their energy levels? Do training and development programmes offer this?
- Does your current supervision structure meet people's needs for learning and personal support as well as meeting managerial needs?
- Are you and your staff clear about the purpose and process of staff meetings and do they meet people's needs?
- Do staff have opportunities for discussing how changes will affect them personally (e.g. outside 'mass' meetings)?
- What opportunities are there for helping staff deal with the inevitable losses stemming from change?

A staff team had undergone so much 'training and development' they had become tired and less enthusiastic about it. When the manager became aware of this she decided to do some brief communication exercises then spend the rest of the day on a long country walk where the team could have time to reflect and chat with one another. Lunch then followed in a pub. It was one of the most effective team-building experiences.

Managers' own agendas

By focusing on their staff, managers may neglect their own needs. Some management teams have found it helpful to take time away from the service and its day-to-day demands to look at what is happening and clarify the way forward.

- What opportunities do you have for reflection and renewal?
- Do you make time to reflect on how change will affect you?
- How will your relationships with staff change as the service changes?

Recruitment

As stated above, staff have been expected to fulfil an increasingly wide range of functions. It may be more effective to separate out some tasks so that not everyone is a keyworker, for example. Having posts with more clearly defined responsibilities can be much more effective.

- What scope is there for redefining posts?
- When a post becomes vacant, do you always consider whether the job description and person specification could be redefined?

A service for 120 people had two hours of speech therapy fortnightly so there was much unmet need. The next time a centre worker's post was vacant the manager advertised for a speech therapist, despite the fact that they were usually only employed by the health service. The job description was tailored to include this specialism and a fully qualified speech therapist duly recruited.

What this means for front-line staff

A service user recently asked: 'Why do people come and work with people with learning disabilities?' This is a question which individual front-line staff could usefully ask themselves. Are they clear about their purpose, about what is expected of them and whether they wish to pursue a career in this direction?

Service development and staff development

Planning how the service can achieve relevant outcomes for users and planning how staff can assist in this is a 'chicken and egg' situation. Which comes first? In fact they are inextricably linked and must fit together in a coherent fashion. If we have clear values and outcomes for users then we'll have a better idea of what staff need to do to achieve these.

Staff will need to learn how to understand the individual people they work with – their aspirations, their gifts, their problems, their families and their ties and connections to the real world outside the day centre. They will also need to know more about the community and how it organises itself if they are to help people find their place there. They will need to become more skilled at helping people overcome their difficulties in becoming part of that world. In summary: staff need to develop the competencies for knowing people, knowing communities, and supporting and safeguarding people.

Service and staff development are like a wheel that rolls continuously. Experience feeds a new round of learning, clarifying values and aims and planning refinements and changes. And so it continues . . .

Useful contacts

Changeover, c/o Scottish Human Services Trust, 1a Washington Court, Washington Lane, Edinburgh EH11 2HA. Freephone 0500 246960.

Changeover is an open learning pack that facilitates change in day centres for people with learning difficulties. Part of the programme involves consultancy, a database of good practice and an information exchange to encourage networking.

Reference

Sawden, C. and D., (1995), Chapter 1, in *Good Practice in Supervision,* ed. Jacki Pritchard. London: Jessica Kingsley.

Chapter 11

Joint commissioning day services

Vision and principles

All commissioning and purchasing of day services, whatever the degree of collaboration with other agencies, should aim to bring about measurable improvements in the lives of people with learning disabilities and lead to enhanced participation in integrated, community-based services.

At the heart of the commissioning task must be a commitment to listening to the wishes of people with learning disabilities, finding out how they want to spend their days and identifying and deploying the resources needed to make this happen through the purchasing task. Purchasers – and particularly those in senior positions – can find it difficult to be in touch with people's lives and experiences, but it is essential if services are to meet users' needs and aspirations.

Joint commissioning is based on the belief that people's needs can be met more effectively and efficiently if agencies work together to identify those needs and determine how best to meet them.

Experience has demonstrated that a key ingredient of joint commissioning is clear agreement between local partners about aims and objectives and how these are to be achieved. It is about translating agreed strategies into action.

Joint commissioning must become part of the organisational fabric – as much as anything this is about a way of viewing the world and how people conduct their working lives.

What are the potential benefits of joint commissioning?

Collaborative approaches to commissioning will not solve all the problems associated with developing new community-based services. It is a means to an end not a universal panacea. However, it can be a useful vehicle for progressing the aims of community care, and achieving greater coherency at a strategic level could help to achieve a more seamless service for individual users. Potential benefits include:

- shared agreement about the priorities for change and how services should be organised and delivered in response to identified needs;
- consideration of individuals' health and social care needs holistically – avoiding or minimising the health/social care divide;
- development of joint person-centred assessments;
- reducing the likelihood of wasteful overlaps and gaps in service responses, thus maximising the use of finite resources and development skills;
- sharing of transitional costs through joint management arrangements.

Although there is, as yet, little definitive evidence that joint commissioning is more effective than single-agency approaches, there are clear indications that certain ingredients are important – some strong roots need to be nurtured (see Fig. 1).

The commissioning cycle

The commissioning cycle (DoH, 1995) provides a framework for describing the different elements of joint commissioning (see Fig. 2).

Strategic framework

- Establish a shared view of the principles underpinning future developments. These should be based on person-centred planning which establishes what individuals want to do during the day.
- Seek political commitment, look for strong leaders and involve all stakeholders in developing the framework.
- Establish shared values and broad strategic objectives, including desirable service models so that there is a common sense of purpose.
- Clarify the roles and responsibilities of individual agencies and the necessary mechanisms.

Fig. 1

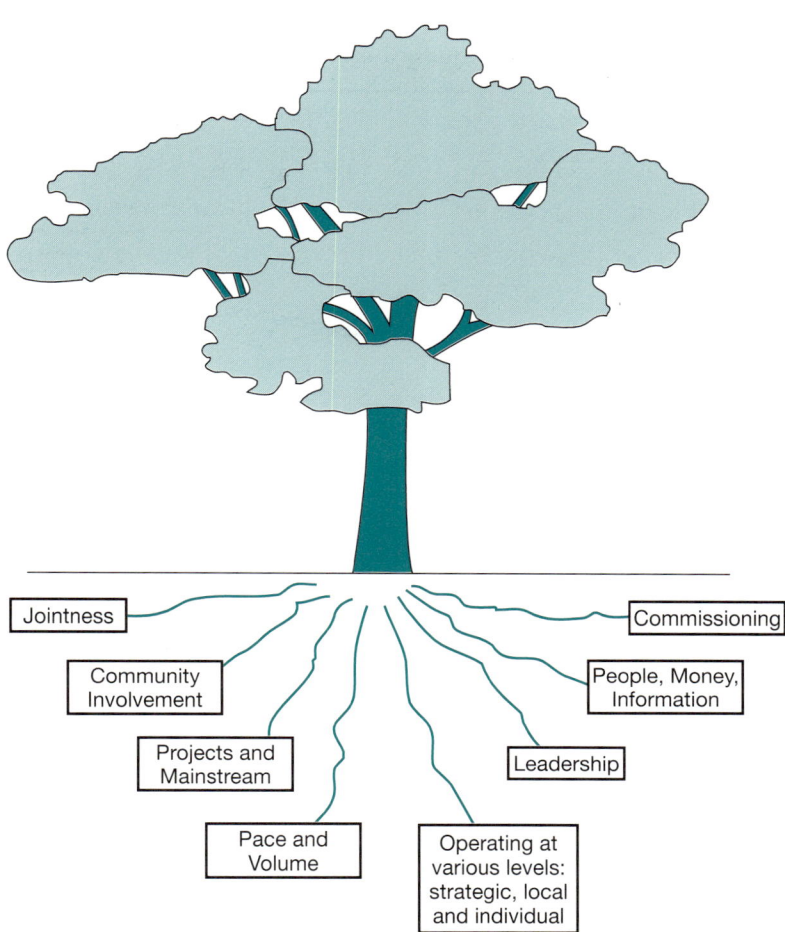

Strategic planning

- Establish an overview of needs in order to inform decisions about priorities and target resources.
- Identify existing services and resources with an emphasis on using mainstream opportunities in the community.
- Define priorities and agree outcomes.
- Consult with users and carers (see below for further discussion of this key element in the cycle).
- Agree commissioning intentions.

Operational planning

- Establish contracting mechanisms.
- Develop quality assurance outcomes which are strongly user-focused.

Fig. 2 The commissioning cycle

- Consult with existing statutory and independent providers.
- Identify gaps and consider how to fill these.
- Ensure the information and related systems are in place to support operational planning, including contracting and provider development activities.

Purchasing activities

- Agree service specifications which ensure flexibility and identify services which offer positive outcomes.
- Select providers, investing in and cultivating those offering best quality services focusing on supported employment, integrated leisure and educational opportunities.
- Identify inefficient use of resources and poor providers and the risks they pose to people using day services.
- Agree contracts and monitoring arrangements.

Monitoring and review

- Collect performance information
- Review providers' performance standards
- Review and/or renegotiate contracts
- Use information obtained to modify the strategic review as necessary.

Operating at various levels

Health and social care commissioners in health and local authorities have statutory responsibilities but there are many other stakeholders whose involvement can be at one or more of three levels:

- Strategic (agency-wide): e.g. commissioning managers, users and carers representatives.
- Local (relating to an area): e.g. team manager, health authority manager.
- Individual: e.g. care manager, advocate, the person concerned.

What this means for users and carers

User and carer involvement is essential because it:

- offers a real opportunity to develop day services which are responsive to users' needs and wishes in line with current community care policies;
- can help ensure that specifications take account of the cultural and religious diversity in local communities;
- can help ensure that services are purchased on the basis of expressed need and that provision is sufficiently flexible to reflect people's changing situations.

What this means for managers

Money matters

Pooled budgets are technically illegal but health authorities can transfer monies to local authorities (NHS Act 1977, S.28a). Local authorities may also have access to health authority or NHS Trust staff who can discharge local authority functions, including incurring expenditure (Local Government Act 1972, S.113). Together with joint agreements on ring-fenced budgets, these offer the best opportunities for inter-agency collaboration on purchasing. Sixty per cent of expenditure on learning disability is within health services even though much of this is needed for social care. This makes collaboration absolutely essential.

Projects and mainstream

Individual projects are generally the best way to make progress. But if these are to have any wider impact (e.g. on overall strategy), they must be properly managed so that experience and knowledge gained by joint working is properly disseminated.

Pace and volume

These two factors have to be balanced. A sense of momentum is important in generating commitment and establishing credibility but if the pace is too rapid and the volume of activity too large it may be difficult to keep all the stakeholders on board.

Leadership

The personal involvement of organisational leaders together with their authorising and empowering of others is crucial. But middle to senior managers are equally important. As 'boundary operators' who understand how both agencies' systems operate they can progress joint commissioning by persuading, cajoling and personal example.

References

Department of Health (1995), *An Introduction to Joint Commissioning.* DoH.

Department of Health (1995), *Practical Guidance on Joint Commissioning for Project Leaders.* DoH.

Gostick, C. (1993), *Collaborative Commissioning: Issues and Objectives.* North West Thames RHA.

Knapp, M. and Wistow, G. (1992), *Joint Commissioning for Community Care.* PSSRU, University of Kent; and Nuffield Institute, University of Leeds.

Poxton, R. (1994/5), *Joint Commissioning Briefing Papers 1–4.* King's Fund.

Waddington, P. (1995), 'Joint commissioning of services for people with learning disabilities: a review of the principles and the practice', *British Journal of Learning Disabilities,* vol. 23.

Wertheimer, A. and Greig, R. (1993), *Report on Joint Commissioning for Community Care.* National Development Team.

Chapter 12

Finance

Vision and principles

For visions to become reality, plans for new daytime opportunities must be cost-effective and affordable to purchasers and providers. If there is thorough financial planning and budgeting from the start, most financial uncertainties can be removed.

From the purchasers' viewpoint, their tightly constrained budgets cannot easily be enhanced, so proposals for reprovisioning will usually need to demonstrate: a financial saving; or a better service at no extra costs; or a better service and a financial saving.

Some thorough and clearly thought-through financial work will be required to demonstrate that these outcomes are achievable. Even if some increased expenditure is possible, rigorous costings will still be important.

Authority members and other decision-makers will only be able to take bold decisions with confidence if adequate financial information is available. From the providers' viewpoint, fees available for providing services must enable them to:

- *operate a service commensurate with their own quality standards;*
- *operate the service at a surplus (or at the very least break-even);*
- *pay salaries sufficient to attract staff with adequate training and experience.*

If fees are too low, either no potential provider will be interested or quality will be unacceptably low.

How do you determine the cost of a new service?

By combining an analysis of existing service budgets with a knowledge of other providers' costs (e.g. independent sector), there should be more than adequate information to draw up accurate estimates of the costs of new services.

The single major cost of any service is staffing. By studying the needs of future service users, operational policies, statutory requirements, etc., it is possible to work out staffing numbers and rotas in draft form. This, together with existing data on salary and benefit levels, enables staff costs to be accurately estimated.

Despite moves towards more dispersed settings, the development of outreach services and greater use of mainstream community facilities, buildings are usually the next biggest cost. Using knowledge of the local property market, building costs, interest rates etc. it is possible to estimate borrowing costs. (If properties are purchased outright the calculation is often simpler.)

The remaining costs – primarily day-to-day running costs and managerial and administrative overheads – can usually be estimated by looking at provision similar to that planned.

By combining the above data a clear financial picture of the service – as it is now and after reprovision – can be prepared.

What happens during the transition period?

Costing a new service accurately is essential but it is equally important to consider the financial impact of the transition since there is almost always an increase in costs while the new service opens and the existing service has not yet closed. The chart opposite illustrates this.

The amount of additional expenditure and the length of time this will take to tail off can be calculated reasonably accurately as long as there are clear plans for:

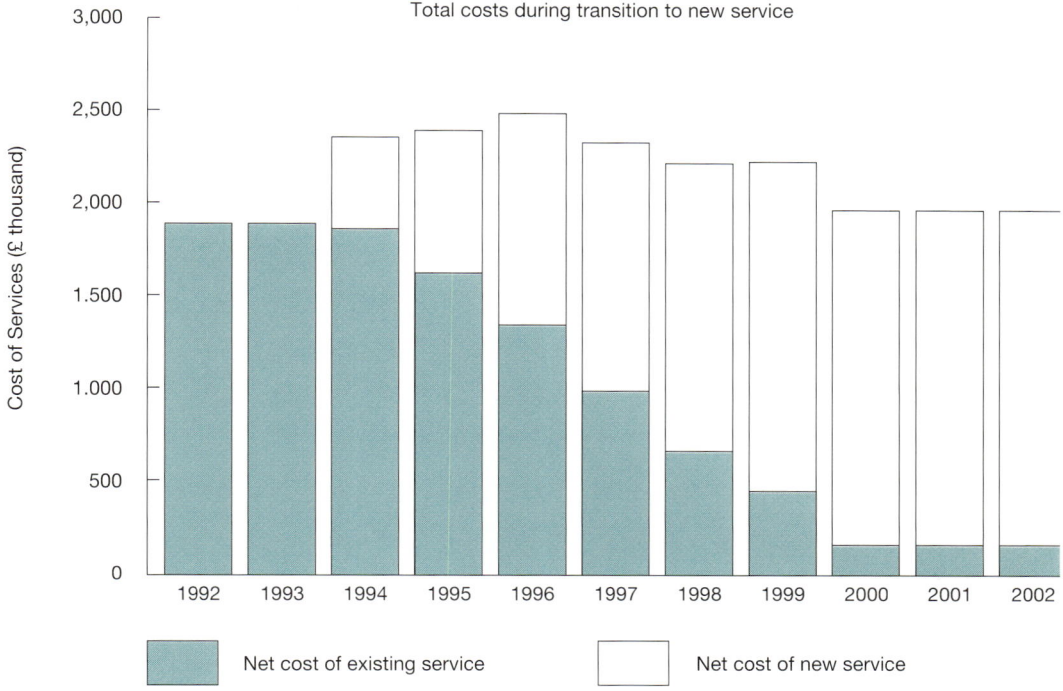

- the timescale of the reprovision programme;
- the order in which people will move from the old service to the new;
- the processes for disposing of old properties.

Why is financial modelling useful?

This method of predicting future financial commitments is often referred to as 'financial modelling' which can best be defined as 'the representation of social phenomena in arithmetical form'.

The most common uses of financial modelling in planning health and social care are:

- to work out the likely costs of planned services;
- to provide a tool to inform and aid negotiations with potential providers so that purchasers tendering for a new service know in advance what is likely to be 'good value for money';
- to predict future demands on services and their likely cost.

Financial modelling for one local authority, undertaken by Rho Delta, provided the forecast shown overleaf. Far from a steady state!

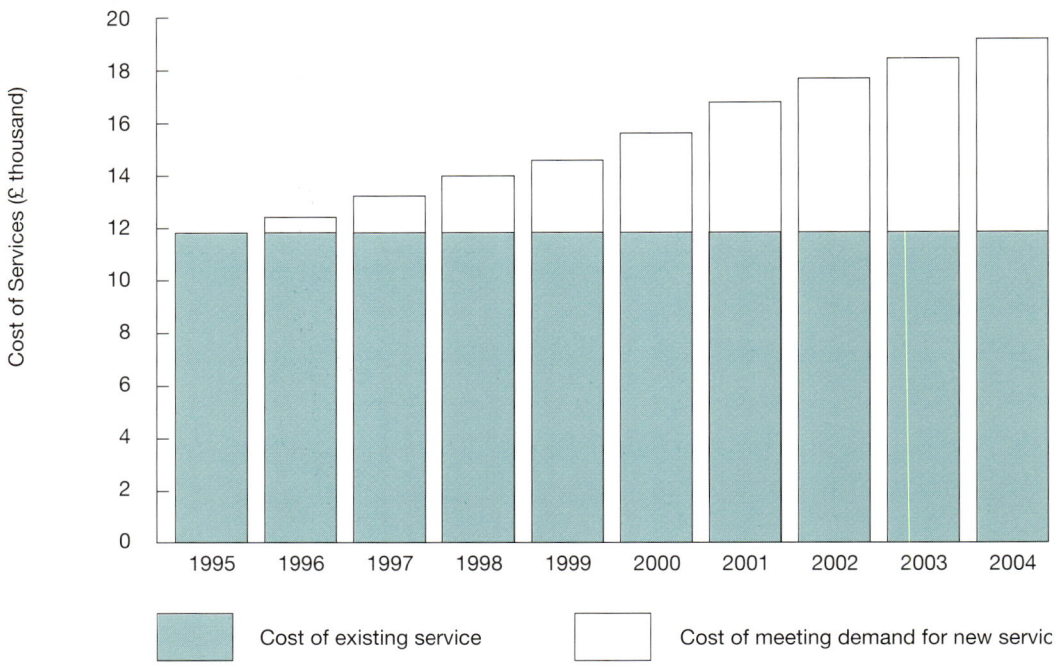

What are the steps in planning a transition?

Careful pre-planning of a reprovision programme can help the programme proceed more smoothly. The following checklist offers a step-by-step schedule.

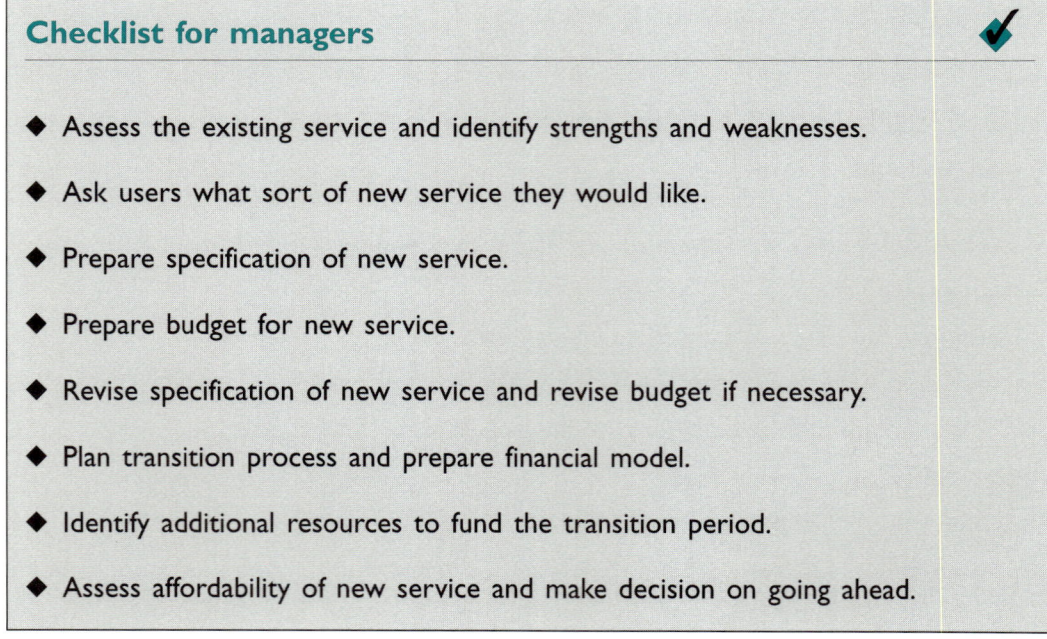

Checklist for managers

◆ Assess the existing service and identify strengths and weaknesses.

◆ Ask users what sort of new service they would like.

◆ Prepare specification of new service.

◆ Prepare budget for new service.

◆ Revise specification of new service and revise budget if necessary.

◆ Plan transition process and prepare financial model.

◆ Identify additional resources to fund the transition period.

◆ Assess affordability of new service and make decision on going ahead.

◆ Invite tenders or expressions of interest from potential providers.

◆ Assess provider bids against budgets.

◆ Negotiate with providers to bring bids in line with budgets.

◆ Award contracts.

Chapter 13

Getting around: creating an accessible environment

Vision and principles

As more and more people with learning disabilities move from a building-based service, where they spend virtually all their time in segregated, purpose-built premises, to a new pattern of daytime opportunities, they will need to find their way round the community and be able to use a much wider range of buildings. More people are likely to be doing this on their own too.

Most people go from place to place many times a day without thinking – from home to work, from work to the shops, from home to the library, to school or the sports centre. People with learning disabilities may need some assistance if they are to move around comfortably in this way.

We need to consider how to reduce the risk to vulnerable individuals by helping them to find their way confidently round the community generally and in places like community or neighbourhood centres, leisure centres and other premises.

Finding your way round the community

We all use signs to help us find our way round, particularly when visiting somewhere for the first time. Subsequently we rely less on those signs, often recognising where we are because we have fixed one or more landmarks (or 'indicators') in our mind – a church, a fast food restaurant, or a phone box, for example.

Whoever is helping the person find their way to a particular venue can use these kinds of indicators to help familiarise them with the route and their eventual destination. It might be possible to tailor the choice of indicators to the particular interests of the user – clothes shops, sports or music outlets, for example. Depending on the individual, the journey can be made repeatedly until the person feels confident that they can find their way round without assistance.

Some of the questions which might help you work out the best route include the following.

- Is the building within easy reach of public transport?
- Does the route have safe road crossings – e.g. zebra crossings, traffic lights, tactile markings underfoot?
- Does the route have changes of direction and are the changes clearly marked?
- Is the route free of confusing repetitions of similar features?
- Is the route wide enough?
- Is it free from hazards such as bollards, concealed exits and buildings features?

Finding one's way round a building

Once a person begins to spend more time in community-based settings they may need to find their way round a number of buildings such as an adult education centre, the local library or the sports centre. This can be relatively straightforward but can also sometimes involve several buildings: a college, for example, may have the canteen in one building and classes in another.

To help a person with learning disabilities get to the right place it may be necessary to think in even more detail than you might for people with other disabilities. For example: when thinking about access to a building you might ask 'Is the door clearly distinguishable from the rest of the front of the building?' For a person with learning disabilities you might need to go further and ask: 'Is the door sufficiently clearly distinguishable from the front of the building to be helpful to that person?'. If the answer is 'No' you will need to think about other elements of the facade of the building. Is there something like a glass lift or a canopy over the door or something else which serves equally well for the person to be able to say: 'I'm in the right place!'.

Each building will be different but the kinds of things which staff might need to check out would be: how the lifts operate; whether the person can find the right toilet (so men do not go into the Ladies and vice versa!); and whether the signs for particular rooms or areas in the building can be understood.

Where a building is being used regularly by people with learning disabilities, service providers might want to consider whether modifications are possible – e.g. adding visual and tactile (Braille) signs for toilets, lifts, and other facilities. Where the building is a general community facility such as a college or leisure centre, this may mean developing a partnership with those owning and operating it. Building managers will realise that these types of modifications will help everyone using the building with the added advantage that staff spend less time giving directions over and over again!

Some of the areas which need to be looked at when finding the best route within a building include: space; light; walls and floors.

Space

- Is there a logical progression of spaces?
- Is there an easy-to-understand way in and out of each space?
- Is it easy to see what each space is used for?
- Do changes in level make the building confusing?

Light

- Is lighting contrast controlled to help orientation and avoid glare?
- Is there highlighting of hazards such as steps and ramps to develop a sense of space?
- Does lighting enhance colour and textural differences?

Walls and floors

- Are differences and similarities in surface textures, colour and tone helpful in getting to know the building?
- Are curves, angles and corners designed to help remember particular areas?
- Are tactile surfaces used?
- Are means of escape distinctive and colour coded?
- Do wall surfaces clarify public and private, safe and dangerous uses?
- Are changes in level emphasised by textural and colour contrasts?
- Is colour/texture contrast used to mark routes and means of escape?

If people with learning disabilities can move around more freely they will have more control over their own lives and access to a greater variety of activities which will enrich their lives and provide more choice.

Useful contact

Centre for Accessible Environments, 60 Gainsford Street, London SE1 2NY.
Tel: 0171 357 8182.

Chapter 14

Transport

Vision and principles

Access to private and public transport is central to increasing people's choices, making their lifestyle more varied and improving the overall quality of their lives. If that seems a bit far-fetched, try listing all the transport options you have to draw on when planning your work, holiday or shopping trips: that will give you a vision of what people with learning disabilities should expect.

Communities, if they exist at all, are spread out. How many people can walk to work, for example? How many people even shop on foot these days? If you look at your own lifestyle and find you are not reliant on the list in Table 1 then the chances are you are a car owner/driver unlike virtually everyone with a learning disability.

Unless transport issues are really taken on board, people using your services are probably being unnecessarily restricted in what they can do and where they can go.

In thinking about transport for people with learning disabilities it is easy to forget that resources are already being spent on this. We forget that people with disabilities have purchasing power which is quite separate from the usual funding source for general transport. Bring these stakeholders together and you have more than the sum of the parts.

The current scene

Many people with learning disabilities have to put up with a 'there and back again' ride to a day centre. During the day, it is probably a lottery whether they get to use the centre's transport. If they do, how about a nice group outing in the brightly painted minibus to help people 'integrate' into the local supermarket perhaps?

Some of the worst current practices include:

- the entire centre budget being used on transporting people to and from the centre every day;
- people having to wait on cold, windy street corners (without even the benefit of a bus shelter) for 'special' transport which is often unreliable;
- bus passes that can't be used until after 9.30 am making it impossible for people to travel to work for free;
- services not having any links with local community transport groups, bus companies or local/national access campaigning groups;
- service users and carers not being asked about their hopes and fears around independent travel and safety issues;
- purchasers refusing to contract out transport to achieve better value for money and a more flexible service.

However, there are some instances of good practice, including the following.

- Flexible purchasing at unit manager or practitioner level.

A day centre manages its own pick-up service using day centre staff as drivers which is not only more flexible but means that cars are available all day as well.

- Flexible purchasing at service user or carer level.
- Direct leasing of vehicles.
- Transport planning groups involving service users and carers, community transport representatives, bus company representatives and independent transport specialists.

The special group set up in one local authority has two carer representatives, one of whom was a professional driver and the other a retired business administrator. Their inside knowledge of contracting, timetabling combined with their knowledge of the needs of carers and service users led to the introduction of door-to-door pick-ups, cancellation of 52-seater coaches and a full service specification for service delivery. Their unique contribution included physically mapping every home address and driving to every venue and residence to check access.

- Competence-based travel training in a clear context, i.e. how to get to work, the swimming pool, the shops tailored to individual's activities.

There are many examples of people with substantial support needs being able to travel safely on known routes to known destinations following comprehensive training, shadowing and fading out of the support person.

- Flexibility so that someone can set out to an activity from home rather than the centre if that is easier.
- Using customer purchasing power to directly negotiate with bus companies or community enterprises set up by users and carers with support from staff.
- Negotiation with local voluntary organisations and carers groups to take on transport provision under contract.

What this means for managers

Managers need to be aware that flexible provision of transport and ensuring everybody has access to comprehensive travel training are essential building blocks in a new, more community-based day service. This chapter offers a range of ideas on how to go about this.

What this means for front-line staff

People's transport needs should be an integral part of individual planning, otherwise there is a danger that they won't be able to participate in activities outside the centre 'because of transport problems'.

When thinking how someone might travel from A to B be as imaginative as possible. Do not assume it has to be either 'special' transport or unassisted use of public transport. There are many options: a local minicab firm may be prepared to do a special deal so that someone can travel unescorted or share a cab, for example. Or there may be retired or unemployed people who would be volunteer drivers in return for the cost of the petrol.

What this means for users

People with learning disabilities have become accustomed to using special transport and being picked up and dropped off at the same time and in the same place every day. Any change may be anxiety-provoking so front-line staff and carers need to be aware of this and offer encouragement and support where necessary.

What this means for carers

Parents may be concerned about safety issues if new transport options other than special coaches or taxis are suggested. These concerns need to be acknowledged and addressed. Travel training will be a waste of time if the person is not then allowed to move around in the community more independently.

Any carers with direct experience of the transport industry could be asked to join a transport working group where their knowledge and expertise would be extremely useful.

This may sound controversial, but some parents who have time and their own transport might consider shared car rotas, volunteer driver schemes and other options which could lessen the need for the transport budget to be spent on simply getting people to and from the day centre. This has been done!

Table 1 Transport options checklist

Bus and train

- Bus passes
- Negotiating new public transport routes by demonstrating customer demand
- Dial-a-Ride
- Escorts on public transport
- Comprehensive travel training (see below)
- Developing special relationships with particular bus companies
- Tendering exercise for local transport companies to a detailed specification drawn up

after full consultation with day service users, carers and staff

- Setting up your own community transport group as a social firm or small business
- Direct negotiations with community transport groups
- Volunteer drivers scheme

Car
- Shared lifts
- Setting up a 'share-a-car' scheme as a social firm or small business
- Taxi cards
- Building special relationships with particular taxi firms and named drivers
- Lease cars, 7 seaters and minibuses for each centre

Comprehensive personal travel training
- Road safety and other 'streetwise' training for safe walking
- Structured training and support to cover use of public transport including shadowing, and volunteer or paid escorts on public transport
- Safe cycle routes and generally cycle safety
- Identity cards as used in outdoor pursuits for added safety and back-up
- Redeployment of centralised transport budgets to individuals and families

---

Useful contacts

Ron Green and Pat Hall (Parent Representatives)
Transport Project Group
London Borough of Havering
The Hermitage
Billet Lane
Hornchurch
RM11 1XL
(Carer involvement in reproviding transport)

Noreen Dunwoodie
Macon House
Macon Way

Crewe
Cheshire
Tel: 01270 582452
(County Transport Group)

DART (Dial-a-Ride and Taxi-Card Users)
25 Leighton Road
London NW5 2QD
Tel: 0171 482 2325
(Campaigning for accessible transport)

Moira Dennison
Mencap National
117 Golden Lane
London EC1Y DRT
Tel: 0171 454 0454
(Transport Information Pack 1995)

Kevin McCall
Southwark Social Services Department
Kennington Workshop
42 Breganza Street
London SE17 3RT
Tel: 0171 820 0457
(Day centre which manages its own transport)

Chapter 15

Legal issues

Vision and principles

People with learning disabilities have a right to expect a range of community care services, including day services.

Good assessment of individual need is essential if people are to have good quality and appropriate services.

The legislation, government guidance and circulars described in this chapter/appendix set out the legal framework within which day services should be properly delivered.

What duties are there to provide day services?

The duty to provide day services is set out in the National Assistance Act 1948, s.29 and in the Local Authority Circular (93)10 Appendix 2.

National Assistance Act 1948

This Act places a duty on the social services department to provide day services for people over 18 living in the local area and described as 'disabled' (which includes people with learning disabilities).

'Disabled' is defined by s.29 of the Act as persons ages 18 or over who are blind, deaf or dumb or who suffer from a mental disorder of any description and either persons aged 18 or over who are substantially and permanently handicapped by illness, injury, congenital deformity or other disabilities as may be described.

Chronically Sick and Disabled Persons Act 1970

This Act also places duties on the local authority to provide services and assess individuals.

Section 1 provides that the local authority must:

– inform themselves of the number of persons entitled to services under s.29 of the National Assistance Act 1948 within their area and assess needs and make arrangements for these people [s.1];
– publish information from time to time on the services provided under s.29 of the National Assistance Act 1948 [s.1(2)(A)];
– inform any user of these services and about any other services which are available and relevant to the person's needs and which the local authority is aware of.

Section 2 provides that where the local authority is satisfied that a person is entitled to services under s.29 of the National Assistance Act and is ordinarily resident in their area the local authority must make arrangements to meet the persons needs in any of the following areas:

– practical assistance at home;
– assistance in obtaining wireless, television, library or similar recreational activities;

– provision of lectures, games, outings or other recreational facilities outside home or assistance in taking advantage of educational facilities which are available;
– help with travel to services approved by the local authority;
– assistance in arranging for adaptations to be carried out in the person's home or the provision of additional facilities for the person's greater safety, comfort or convenience;
– help with holidays where the local authority or other person provides these;
– meals at home or elsewhere;
– help in getting a telephone or any special equipment to use the telephone.

How are these services to be provided for people with learning disabilities?

The local authority has legal duties to assess a person's needs and then state what services will be provided for that person. These duties are set out in the Disabled Persons (Services Consultation and Representation) Act 1986 and the NHS and Community Care Act 1990.

Disabled Persons (Services Consultation and Representation) Act 1986

Section 4 states that a local authority has a duty to consider the needs of the disabled person when asked to do so by:

– the disabled person; or
– a carer who is not employed by a local authority.

The Act also requires the local authority to assess for community care services young people about to leave full-time education. Section 6 states that this assessment must be done within five months of the local education authority giving notice that a person is leaving full-time education. This notice must be given eight months before the person actually leaves full-time education.

National Health Service and Community Care Act 1990

Under this Act the local authority must:

– assess a person's needs for community care services to assess which services the person needs;
– provide a formal complaints procedure for service users and others;

– publish a community care plan for its area every year and consult the community about this plan.

NB This Act is about the assessment of individual needs and provides no new services. The care manager, employed by the local authority, will arrange the assessment, and services will usually be provided by private and voluntary organisations.

What does the assessment mean?

Section 47 of the NHS and Community Care Act 1990 states that:

'where it appears to a local authority that any person for whom they may provide or arrange for the provision of community care services may be in need of such services, the authority:

(a) shall carry out an assessment of his need for these services; and
(b) having regard to the result of that assessment shall then decide whether his needs call for the provision by them of any such services'.

The definition of 'need' in this context is discussed below.

Section 47 (5)(6) gives the right for services to be provided to users before an assessment is made where there is urgent need (e.g. family breakdown or other unusual or difficult circumstances).

How should assessments be carried out?

Each local authority has its own assessment procedure and written information about the procedure and relevant documentation is usually available.

Unless social services initiates the assessment, the person with learning disabilities or their carer should request an assessment. Social services will then decide whether to carry this out.

If an assessment is offered, a care manager will be appointed and the person, their carer and other relevant people will be consulted.

A proper assessment of needs should include:

- accommodation;
- health care;
- personal care;
- social needs, including day services;
- employment;
- education;
- finance;
- the needs of the carer.

Other important points about assessment:

- social services should co-operate with health and housing authorities where this is relevant to the assessment: social services must 'invite them to assist' (NHS and Community Care Act 1990, s.47(3));
- a community care assessment must be reviewed and updated regularly;
- if the person or their carer feels his or her needs have changed a reassessment should be requested;
- if social services are already providing someone with services, these cannot be withdrawn until a reassessment has been carried out.

What is a need?

The NHS and Community Care Act 1990 does not define 'need' though some explanation is included in the Government circular *Care Management and Assessment; Summary of Practice Guidance,* which states that needs are:

'requirements of individuals to enable them to achieve, maintain or restore an acceptable level of social independence or quality of life as defined by the particular care agency or authority'.

The local authority's annual community care plan will also explain what a 'need' is. Most will also publish 'eligibility criteria' defining how needs are addressed in individual areas.

Do identified needs have to be met?

In a recent High Court case it was stated that social services are entitled to take into account resources when deciding what services to provide. However, the individual's identified needs are most important and the High Court also said that resource considerations should be only 'one factor'.

Is it possible to challenge local authority decisions?

It may be possible to challenge social services' decisions about assessment and/or assessments if:

- the local authority refuses to carry out an assessment and this is thought to be unreasonable; (NB the local authority is entitled to consider resources and prioritising of need);
- the local authority does not give either good reasons or any reasons for failing to carry out an immediate assessment;
- the service user disagrees with the delay in conducting the assessment and there is unreasonable delay in carrying this out;
- the local authority defines need as based on available resources rather than on the needs of the individual;
- the social services department fails to fulfil its duties and powers to provide community care.

Since implementation of the NHS and Community Care Act 1990, the courts have established some principles relating to what the local authority must do. Local authorities must:

- enquire about all relevant factors;
- give applicants an opportunity to explain their circumstances;
- be responsible for making proper enquiries;
- not reject medical evidence out of hand without further enquiry.

When an assessment is challenged, the service user may wish to ask for an independent assessment by a professional such as a doctor, psychiatrist or social worker acting independently from the local authority.

How can the local authority be challenged?

Using the local authority complaints procedure

This is enshrined in the Local Authority Social Services Act 1970 s.7(b), Local Authority Social Services (Complaints Procedure) Order 1990 and the Complaints Procedure Directions 1990.

Local authorities are required to publish information about the procedure and to have a designated complaints officer.

The procedure has three stages:

- *informal stage:* social services should try to resolve the complaint with the care manager, service user and other relevant people.
- *formal stage:* if the complaint cannot be resolved informally, social services must send the complainant details of the formal and review stages of the procedure and ask the person to submit a written complaint. All written complaints must be registered and responded to within three months of receipt. An initial reply should be given within 28 days. Although this is a written procedure the complainant may also wish to meet social service managers to explain the problem.
- *review stage:* any complainant not satisfied with the outcome of the second stage can ask for a panel review. This request must be made within 28 days of the complainant receiving the results of the the formal stage. The panel must meet within 28 days of receiving the request. The complainant has the right of representation although this should not be a barrister or solicitor acting in a professional capacity.

Making a complaint to the local authority monitoring officer

The monitoring officer, appointed under s.5 of the Local Government and Housing Act 1989, must report to the authority on any proposal, decision or omission made by the authority in any of its committees or by officers which has given rise to or is likely to give rise to:

(a) a contravention of law or any code of practice made or approved by or under any enactment, or
(b) maladministration or injustice as would fall within the investigative remit of the local government ombudsman.

The monitoring officer must consult with the local authority's chief executive and chief finance officer and a report must be sent to all members of the authority who have responsibility for the decision.

Making a complaint to the local government ombudsman

The ombudsman can investigate any complaint against a local authority where there has been 'maladministration' causing injustice to the complainant, including:

- unreasonable delay;
- bias or unfairness;
- failure to follow proper procedures;
- poor standards of decision-making;
- incompetence.

Other important points to note:

- this procedure is slow but has the advantage of being independent;
- a person can complain directly to the ombudsman or can ask a local councillor to complain on their behalf;
- complaints should be made in writing;
- the ombudsman will not investigate if legal proceedings have started;
- the ombudsman can require the local authority to disclose all relevant information;
- the ombudsman can recommend awarding compensation.

Taking legal action

Any service user considering legal action should obtain legal advice as soon as possible.

Legal aid may be available under the Green Form scheme and/or the civil legal aid system. Information about entitlement can be obtained from a law centre or legal aid solicitor.

One form of legal action is to apply for a judicial review. This is an application to the High Court, asking a judge to review an action or decision made by a local authority or secretary of state.

When reviewing whether an action or decision was properly taken the judge will consider:

- illegality;
- irrationality;
- procedural impropriety.

A person can challenge decisions about the following areas of community care:

- quality of assessments;
- provision of services;
- charges for services;
- the complaints procedure and other powers and duties of the secretary of state.

Applications for judicial review should usually be made within three months of the decision which is being challenged. The court has discretion to extend the time limit but only with good reason.

An action to sue for damages may be possible: if a local authority has failed to provide services to an individual and where the individual has suffered damage. This is a private action. The law in this area is complicated so legal advice must be sought without delay.

The default power of the secretary of state may be activated. The secretary of state for health has power to step in when a local authority fails to comply with its statutory community care duties. This has not yet happened but it is still possible to make a complaint to the office of the Secretary of State.

A person with learning difficulties may wish to take any of the above legal actions at the same time. It is important to seek legal advice from experienced solicitors. The Community Care Practitioners Group can refer cases and can be contacted through the Law Society, 115 Chancery Lane, London WC1. Tel: 0171 242 1222.

Note: Charging for services

Local authorities may charge for services, including day services, under s.17 of the Health and Social Services and Social Security Adjudications Act 1983. Charges must be reasonable and must not exceed what is reasonably practicable for the person to pay.

Appendix: other useful organisations

Camden Society for People with Learning Disabilities Training and Employment Services

This well-established voluntary organisation provides a range of housing, outreach support, social, training and employment services to people with learning disabilities in the London Borough of Camden (and now in other areas of London). Several people with learning disabilities are employed within the organisation.

The Camden Society aims to provide employment opportunities through projects which are relevant to the needs of the local community; and by ensuring that trainees familiarise themselves with the demands of open employment. A wide network of employers has been developed giving access to a range of employment and job trials.

Current employment and training projects include:

- a café offering sheltered employment and work opportunities;
- two other cafés which act as catering training projects;
- a business mailing service and a gardening service, both offering sheltered employment.

About 15 people each year successfully transfer from sheltered to open employment and are offered continuing support to ensure successful outcomes.

The Camden Society aims to develop its services as follows:

- to obtain contracts with local authorities in other areas to help them develop similar services;
- to offer a consultancy to other providers hoping to develop similar services;
- to expand the range of income-generating activities within the society's existing services (e.g. an outside catering service).

Camden Society for People with Learning Difficulties, 245 Royal College Street, London NW1 9LT. Tel: 0171 485 8177.

Rho Delta

Rho Delta is an established consultancy service offering a wide range of financial, strategic and technical support. Most of their work is with clients in the statutory, voluntary and independent sectors who are involved in the purchasing and provision of housing, social services and health care.

Rho Delta brings together experienced consultants from local government, health authorities and leading voluntary sector agencies involved in the provision of housing and personal support services. They assist clients to develop a variety of practical and realistic solutions to the challenges they face.

Rho Delta, Merlin House, 122/126 Kilburn High Road, London NW6 4HY. Tel: 0171 372 3989; fax: 0171 328 0933.

Community Options Inc. (UK)

Community Options is an internationally based not-for-profit charity. The mission of the organisation is to develop housing and employment for people with disabilities. It offers a variety of supports to individuals with learning difficulties as well as to organisations in need of expertise in housing, educational inclusion, early intervention services, respite model development, changing segregated day service provision to supported employment and facilitating hospital closures.

Community Options has a noted track-record throughout the USA of developing, staffing and maintaining housing for people with physical and severe learning difficulties. Community Options works with various organisations to convert day centres into supported employment and entrepreneurial models. This includes consulting on the installation of business advisory groups to promote employment opportunities. Community Options trains staff in job development, job coaching and techniques to ensure people are integrated into the work environment.

Community Options has placed over 750 persons with severe learning difficulties into supported employment.

Community Options is noted as a hands-on organisation and has extensively assisted agencies with programme planning and development for employment opportunities for people with severe learning difficulties, physical disabilities and mental health problems, using a variety of schemes, rehabilitation technology and training.

Contact: Robert Stack, Community Options Inc., 5 Third Street, Bordertown, New Jersey 08505, USA. Tel: 011 609 298 3455

Further reading

Allen, D (1990). Evaluation of a community-based service for people with profound mental handicaps and additional special needs. *Mental Handicap Research* 3(2):179–85.

Baker, L and Brown, J (1993). *Training in the Social Economy - an evaluation of the European Social Fund training programme managed by the Industrial Common Ownership Movement under objectives 3 and 4.* Leeds: Industrial Common Ownership Movement.

Bedfordshire County Council, Social Services Department (1993). *'People First!': Creating and developing valued day opportunities for adults with a learning disability. A report from a consultation workshop held at Kempson Centre, Saturday 25 September, 1993.*

Beyer, S and Crowe, J (1992). Creating valued day opportunities. *Llais* 26:7–13.

Beyer, S., Kilsby, M and Lowe, K (1995). What do ATCs offer in Wales? A survey of Welsh day services. *Mental Handicap Research* 7(1):16–40.

Brandon, D (1993). Money for a change? *Community Living* 7(1): 24–6.

Department of Health (1992). *Social Care for Adults with Learning Disabilities (mental handicap).* LAC(92)15.

Kilsby, M and Beyer, S (1993). Supported employment: the fragile truth. *Llais* 28:14–17. Cardiff: SCOVO.

Lart, R (1993). Inside adult day care. *Community Care* 994; (25 November 1993 Suppl.).

Le Touze, S and Pahl, J (1990). *A consumer survey among people with learning disabilities in Kent.* University of Kent at Canterbury - Centre for Health Studies.

Lowe, K, Beyer, S, Kilsby, M and Felce, D (1993). Activities and engagement in day services for people with a mental handicap. *Journal of Intellectual Disability Research* 36:489–503.

McConkey, R, Walsh, PN, Conneally, S (1993). Neighbours' reactions to community service: contrasts before and after services open in their locality. *Mental Handicap Research* 6(2):131–41.

National Development Team (1993). *Survey of supported employment services in England, Wales and Scotland.* London: NDT.

National Development Group for the Mentally Handicapped (1977). *Day Services for Mentally Handicapped Adults.* Pamphlet 5. London: HMSO.

O'Bryan, A and O'Brien, J (1995). *Supported employment quality assurance.* Manchester: NDT.

Porterfield, J and Gathercole, C (1985).*The Employment of People with Mental Handicap: Progress towards an ordinary working life.* Project Paper No. 55. London, King's Fund.

Pozner, A and Brown, J (1994). *Survey of Supported Employment.* Research Series No.17. London: Department of Employment.

Puddicombe, B (1992). *Days: in search of real alternatives to the Adult Training Centre.* London: Values into Action.

Rose, ., Davis, C and Gotch, L (1993). A comparison of the services provided to people with profound and multiple disabilities in two different day centres. *British Journal of Developmental Disabilities* Part 2(77):83–94.

Shaw, I, Williamson, H and Parry-Langdon, N (1992). Developing models for day services.*Social Policy and Administration* 26(1):73–86.

Sutcliffe, J (1994). The Further and Higher Education Act 1992 and adults with learning difficulties. *British Journal of Learning Disability* 22(3):82–4.

Welsh Mental Handicap Advisory Panel (1995). *Include Me In! How people with learning disabilities can lead a fuller life outside their home.* Cardiff: Welsh Office.

Wertheimer, A (ed.) (1991). *Making It Happen: Employment opportunities for people with severe learning difficulties.* London: King's Fund Centre.

Wertheimer, A (1992). *Real Jobs: Report of a conference for supported employment agencies, 26 July 1991.* London: NDT.

Wertheimer, A. 1992. *Real Jobs Initiative 1990–92: An evaluation.* London:NDT.

Woolrich, R. (ed.) (1990). *Developing Day Services.* Ross on Wye: Association of Professions for Mentally Handicapped People.